52 Things Jesus Did For You

Meditate Through the Death, Burial, and Resurrection of Jesus – One Truth at a Time

Equipping You to Pray from His Finished Work

Clint Byars

Copyright

© 2025 Clint Byars. All rights reserved.

ISBN: 979-8-9913215-3-2

No part of this publication may be reproduced, stored in a retrieval system, or transmitted in any form or by any means —electronic, mechanical, photocopy, recording, or otherwise —without the prior written permission of the publisher, except in the case of brief quotations used in articles or reviews.

Written by Clint Byars, Lead Pastor of Forward Church (www.clintbyars.com)

Unless otherwise indicated, all content—including devotional reflections, prayers, affirmations, and commentary—was authored by Clint Byars.

Published in the United States of America.

Scripture Citations

Scripture quotations marked NKJV are taken from the *New King James Version®*. Copyright © 1982 by Thomas Nelson. Used by permission. All rights reserved.

Scripture quotations marked NIV are taken from the *Holy Bible, New International Version®*. NIV®. Copyright © 1973, 1978, 1984, 2011 by Biblica, Inc.™ Used by permission. All rights reserved worldwide.

Scripture quotations marked NLT are taken from the *Holy Bible, New Living Translation*, copyright © 1996, 2004, 2015 by Tyndale House Foundation. Used by permission of Tyndale House Publishers, Inc., Carol Stream, Illinois 60188. All rights reserved.

Scripture quotations marked CSB are taken from the *Christian Standard Bible®, Copyright © 2017, 2020 by Holman Bible Publishers*. Used by permission. Christian Standard Bible® and CSB® are federally registered trademarks of Holman Bible Publishers.

Scripture quotations marked ESV are taken from *The Holy Bible, English Standard Version®. ESV® Text Edition: 2016.* Copyright © 2001 by Crossway, a publishing ministry of Good News Publishers. Used by permission. All rights reserved.

CONTENTS

Introduction		1
1.	In the Beginning Was the Word	5
2.	He Became Like Us in Every Way	8
3.	He Lived a Perfect Human Life	11
4.	He Chose Obedience for My Redemption	14
5.	He Endured the Cross for Joy	17
6.	He Became Sin So I Could Be Righteous	20
7.	He Became the Curse to Redeem Me	23
8.	He Nailed the Law's Accusation to the Cross	26
9.	He Bore My Sickness and Disease so I can Be Healed	29
10.	He Was Punished for My Peace	32
11.	He Was Crushed for My Iniquities	35
12.	The Punishment That Brought Me Peace Was Upon Him	38
13.	By His Stripes I Am Healed	41

14. He Was Oppressed and Afflicted
    for My Freedom   44

15. He Was Judged Guilty
    So I Could Be Justified   47

16. He Was Cut Off
    So I Could Be Brought Near   50

17. He Was Buried in a Rich Man's
    Tomb to Fulfill the Word   53

18. He Descended Into Hades
    So I'd Never Be Forsaken   56

19. He Was Raised Because
    He Remained Faithful in Death   59

20. He Overcame the Power of Death   62

21. He Ascended with His Own Blood
    to Secure Eternal Redemption   65

22. He Removed My Sinful Nature
    and Gave Me a New Heart   68

23. He United Me with God by His Spirit   71

24. He Made Me His Temple   74

25. He Gave Me the Right to Be God's Child   77

26. He Promised Me an Inheritance
    as His Child   80
27. I Am a Joint Heir with Christ   83
28. He Made Me an Ambassador
    of His Kingdom   86
29. He Put His Spirit In
    and Upon Me for Power   89
30. He Sends Me to the World to Glorify God   92
31. He Gave Me Eternal Life   95
32. He Died So I Can Live   98
33. He Took Away My Shame   101
34. He Removed the Record of My Wrongs   104
35. He Made Me Righteous   107
36. He Reconciled Me to God   110
37. He Made Me Holy and Blameless   113
38. He Gave Me His Own Righteousness   116
39. He Qualified Me to Share in
    His Inheritance   119
40. He Delivered Me from Darkness   122
41. He Gave Me the Light of Life   125

42.	He Broke the Power of Fear	128
43.	He Took My Punishment So I Could Have Peace	131
44.	He Gave Me His Victory Over the World	134
45.	He Gave Me the Power to Overcome Sin	137
46.	He Gave Me a New Identity	140
47.	He Gave Me Bold Access to the Father	143
48.	He Gave Me the Mind of Christ	146
49.	He Seated Me in Heavenly Places	149
50.	He Gave Me the Ministry of Reconciliation	152
51.	He Made Me a Vessel of His Glory	155
52.	He Will Glorify Me with Him Forever	158

INTRODUCTION

Welcome to *52 Things Jesus Did for You*—a transformational journey designed to reveal the depth, detail, and beauty of what Jesus accomplished through His life, death, resurrection, ascension, and glorification. This book is not just a theological summary—it's an invitation into transformation. With each of the 52 truths, you'll walk through the very heart of the gospel, one promise at a time, and learn to put on the new man—your true identity in Christ.

WHO IS JESUS

Jesus is the Word made flesh (John 1:14), fully God and fully human. He is the Logos—the divine expression, reason, and blueprint of God Himself. Through Him all things were made (John 1:3), and in Him all things hold together (Colossians 1:17). He is not only the agent of creation but the very substance of it. Everything that exists flows from His voice, His presence, and His person.

The Word of God is not just a message—it's a Person. And that Person now lives in you. His Word is alive in your heart and in your mouth (Romans 10:8), and it is powerfully transformative. When you speak the truth of who He is and what He's done—when you feel it, declare it, meditate on it—it renews your soul, aligns your thoughts with heaven, and transforms your inner world.

Jesus is not only Savior—He is King, Intercessor, Healer, and Firstborn among many brothers and sisters. Everything He did, He did for *you*. Not just to rescue you—but to raise you into a new life and place you inside His eternal story.

THE POWER OF MEDITATION

Meditation is not a mystical ritual—it's a biblical discipline. God told Joshua to meditate in His Word day and night so he could prosper and succeed (Joshua 1:8). David delighted in meditating on God's law because it brought him wisdom, clarity, and strength (Psalm 1, Psalm 119).

You were created to be transformed by what you behold. Neuroscience now confirms what Scripture has always said: your brain is plastic—it can be changed. Your thoughts carve neural pathways, and your beliefs shape your reality. That means transformation is not only spiritual—it's physiological. And the source you meditate on matters deeply.

This devotional is designed to help you plant truth intentionally. Each entry invites you to read it, speak it, feel it, visualize it, and act on it when inspired by the Spirit. These are not abstract promises—they are living seeds. And your heart is fertile ground.

WHO YOU ARE NOW

In Him, you are a new creation (2 Corinthians 5:17). You are forgiven, redeemed, healed, made righteous, adopted, seated in heavenly places, filled with the Spirit, and destined for glory. You are not trying to become holy—you are already made holy in Christ. You are not earning love—you are already deeply loved. Your new identity is not based on your behavior but on your union with Jesus.

HOW TO USE THIS BOOK

Each entry is built around a single accomplishment of Jesus. You'll find:

- A **Scripture** that anchors the truth

- A personal **Explanation** of what Jesus did and how it affects your life

- A bold, present-tense **Affirmation** to renew your mind

- A heartfelt **Prayer** to engage your spirit

- A **Reflection (Leaven)** that invites the truth to work into your heart like yeast in dough

- And **Three Reflection Questions** to help you put on the new man in real time

You can read each entry at the start of your week and revisit it throughout the days that follow. Speak the affirmation out loud. Sit with the prayer. Let the leaven of the Word change the way you think, feel, and live.

This is more than a devotional—it's a discipleship guide. It's a training manual for the heart. It's a quiet revolution of grace working its way into your soul.

YOUR TRANSFORMATIONAL JOURNEY

As you move through these 52 transformations truths, you'll walk a path that begins with Christ's incarnation and ends with your eternal glorification in Him. You'll see how every part of His story was designed to redeem every part of yours.

Let this journey persuade your heart of who Jesus really is—and who you now are because of Him. Let the details of what He did become the foundations of how you think, how you pray, how you love, and how you live.

Welcome to the journey.
Welcome to transformation.
Welcome to your life in Christ.

1

THE WORD BECAME FLESH

John 1:1 (NASB) In the beginning was the Word, and the Word was with God, and the Word was God.

John 1:14 (NLT) So the Word became human and made his home among us. He was full of unfailing love and faithfulness. And we have seen his glory, the glory of the Father's one and only Son.

Before anything existed—before time, creation, or humanity—the Logos already was. Jesus is the eternal Logos, present with God and fully God. He is not an afterthought or merely a prophet; He is the very expression of God's mind, logic, character, and nature, sent to dwell among us.

Hebrews 2:9 But we see him who for a little while was made lower than the angels, namely Jesus, crowned with glory and honor because of the suffering of death, so that by the grace of God he might taste death for everyone. ESV

When the Logos became flesh, He didn't just appear as a human—He fully entered into our experience.

The eternal Word took on our humanity to bring us into His divinity.

He is the bridge between the eternal God and us. Through Him, we see the Father's glory, wrapped in love and truth. This wasn't just a visit—it was an incarnation of purpose, to reveal God and redeem us.

Because the Word became flesh, we now have access to everything that He is. Colossians 2:9 (NKJV) says, "For in Him dwells all the fullness of the Godhead bodily; 10 and you are complete in Him." That means His fullness has a direct effect on us. We are now complete in Him—not lacking, not rejected, not unfinished. The same Word that created the world is the One who remade us when we believed and he's made us great and precious promises so we could be partakers of His divine nature.

Hebrews 2:14 Since therefore the children share in flesh and blood, he himself likewise partook of the same things, that through death he might destroy the one who has the power of death, that is, the devil

Affirmation: I believe that Jesus is the eternal Word, the divine expression of God's heart. He was with God from the beginning and is God Himself. My life is anchored in His truth, shaped by His voice, and sustained by His power.

Prayer: Jesus, You are the eternal Word—God from the beginning, made flesh for me. You came into my world, wrapped Yourself in humanity, and brought heaven with You. You are the glory of the Father, full of love and truth—and You brought that glory to me. Because I am in You, I am complete. I lack nothing. Your love and truth now live in me.

You made my heart Your home. You know my pain, and You rescued me from sin. I worship You—not as a distant God, but as the Word made near. Shape everything in me with Your truth. Let Your presence transform how I see myself. You became like me so I could become like You. You are the beginning of all things—including my new life—and I let that rise in my heart like leaven. Amen.

2

HE BECAME LIKE ME IN EVERY WAY

Hebrews 2:17 (CSB) Therefore, he had to be like his brothers and sisters in every way, so that he could become a merciful and faithful high priest in matters pertaining to God, to make atonement for the sins of the people.

Jesus didn't skip the hard parts of being human. He came in humility to dwell with us. He wasn't insulated from suffering or detached from pain. He entered right into the heart of our broken world, fully embracing the frailty of human life. He felt hunger and thirst. He grew tired. He experienced frustration, sorrow, and deep grief. He wept at the tomb of a friend. He endured betrayal, rejection, and abandonment. He was misunderstood, falsely accused, and humiliated.

He didn't fast-forward through our experience—He absorbed it. And He did it not just for theological necessity, but for *you*. For me. Because love compelled Him to draw near.

Jesus became like us in every way—not just physically, but emotionally and mentally. He faced every kind of temptation but never yielded. He carried the emotional weight of being misunderstood by His own family. He bore the mental anguish of anticipating the cross. He endured spiritual torment in the garden as He sweat drops of blood. And obeyed the Father, even unto death.

Hebrews 4:15 (NIV) says, "For we do not have a high priest who is unable to empathize with our weaknesses, but we have one who has been tempted in every way, just as we are—yet he did not sin." That means Jesus *knows*. Not from a distance, but from the inside. He knows what it's like to be you. He knows the weight of sorrow, the ache of waiting, the sting of injustice. And because He remained sinless, He offered Himself as the perfect representative for all of humanity.

Jesus is not a distant Savior. He is not an untouchable King. He is Immanuel—*God with us*. He took on flesh and walked our streets. He entered our suffering to redeem it. He knows your weaknesses, and yet He never turns away. He stands before the Father on your behalf, not with judgment, but with mercy. Not with condemnation, but with compassion.

He is merciful. He is faithful. He sees you. He understands you. And He still chose to be your High Priest, forever.

Affirmation: Jesus stepped fully into my humanity so He could redeem every part of me. He understands my weaknesses, my struggles, and my pain. I am never alone—He gets me, and He's with me.

Prayer: Jesus, You became like me in every way so You could represent me before God. You didn't avoid my pain—you entered into it. You walked through this life with purity and compassion, and now You stand in my place as my faithful High Priest. You understand me. You empathize with me. You love me. And I am fully known and fully covered by Your mercy.

Thank You for choosing to experience life as I do. Thank You for making atonement for my sins, for being merciful and faithful, and for never being far from me. There is no weakness in me You cannot sympathize with, no part of my story You do not understand. You are my High Priest forever, and I rest in Your compassion. You know me completely—and You still saved me. Amen.

3

HE LIVED A PERFECT LIFE FOR ME

1 Peter 2:22 (NLT) He never sinned, nor ever deceived anyone.

Hebrews 7:26 (NIV) Such a high priest truly meets our need—one who is holy, blameless, pure, set apart from sinners, exalted above the heavens.

Jesus lived the only truly perfect human life. From the moment He entered the world to His final breath, He never sinned—not in word, not in thought, not in action. He was tempted in every way, just as we are, but He never gave in. He kept His heart pure, His motives clean, and His obedience unwavering. He fulfilled every demand of the law with flawless integrity, walking in complete union with the Father.

But His perfection wasn't just for show. It wasn't just to prove that holiness was possible in flesh and blood. It was for you. His perfect life wasn't merely an example to admire—it was a qualification for your salvation. Because He lived without sin, He could become all of yours. Because He fulfilled the law, He could redeem those who failed it. He stood where you couldn't stand, and then offered Himself as the substitute you didn't deserve but desperately needed.

Romans 5:19 (NKJV) declares, "For as by one man's disobedience many were made sinners, so also by one Man's obedience many will be made righteous." Every time Jesus resisted temptation, every time He chose love over retaliation, truth over compromise, humility over pride—He was actively securing your righteousness. It wasn't just the nails that saved you—it was His whole life of spotless obedience.

You are not made righteous because you perform well or avoid failure. You are made righteous because Jesus lived perfectly in your place. His record has become your record. His obedience has been credited to your account. That means your identity is no longer rooted in how well you behave, but in how fully He obeyed. Jesus' perfection isn't something you strive to copy—it's something you receive. His Spirit now lives in you. His righteousness is your new foundation. You are not defined by your worst moments. You are defined by His faithfulness. You are not trying to earn your place—you are learning to live from the place He already secured.

Let that truth rise in you. Let it quiet shame and dismantle performance. Let it fill you with gratitude. Because of Jesus' life, you can now live truly alive.

Affirmation: Jesus lived the life I never could—flawless, faithful, and fully obedient to the Father. His perfect life was exchanged for mine, and now I stand before God as if I had never sinned.

Prayer: Jesus, You lived the perfect life I never could. You walked in full obedience—sinless, pure, and faithful—and You did it for me. You didn't just die in my place, You lived in my place. Your righteousness is now mine. Because of Your obedience, I am accepted, loved, and made right with God.

I don't have to strive to earn what You've already given. I am not defined by my past mistakes or present shortcomings. I am defined by Your perfection. Your obedience covers my disobedience. Your faithfulness makes me whole. Let that truth rise in me like leaven—quietly, steadily, powerfully—reshaping how I see myself. Let my life reflect Your goodness, not because I have to prove anything, but because I'm living from what You've already done. Amen.

4

HE CHOSE OBEDIENCE FOR MY REDEMPTION

Philippians 2:8 (ESV) And being found in human form, he humbled himself by becoming obedient to the point of death, even death on a cross.

Jesus didn't face the cross as a victim of circumstance or pressure—He embraced it with full awareness and willing surrender. He wasn't coerced. He wasn't trapped. He chose. And His choice was obedience—obedience driven by love. From the throne of heaven, He stepped into flesh, walked through suffering, and yielded Himself completely to the Father's will—not just to fulfill prophecy, but to redeem you.

Romans 5:18 (NKJV) says, "Therefore, as through one man's offense judgment came to all men, resulting in condemnation, even so through one Man's righteous act the free gift came to all men, resulting in justification of life." One man's disobedience brought death; Jesus' obedience opened the floodgates of life. He didn't just live obediently—He died obediently. His entire life crescendoed in that one final act of surrender at the cross, and it changed everything for you.

Hebrews 10:9 says, "Then he said, 'Here I am, I have come to do your will.'" That heart posture defined Jesus' entire mission. He chose the Father's will at every turn—for you. Each time He denied His own comfort, held His tongue, forgave His accusers, or pressed through rejection, it was obedience on your behalf. And that obedience now stands in your place. You no longer live under the weight of judgment. His obedience has justified you.

And here's the miracle: His obedience wasn't just an act done for you—it's now a living force within you. Romans 5:19 says, "By one Man's obedience many will be made righteous." His yes became your new nature. His surrender became your strength. You are no longer a slave to sin or performance. You are free —freely loved, freely justified, freely alive.

Let that truth take root in you: Jesus chose obedience with your face in mind. His love led Him to surrender, and His surrender led you to freedom. That obedience is not just history—it's power in you today.

Affirmation: Jesus surrendered His own desires so I could live in the will of God. His obedience empowers me to trust the Father's heart, even when it's hard. I walk in His example of surrender.

Prayer: Jesus, You chose obedience for me. You didn't hesitate, retreat, or resist the Father's will. You humbled Yourself in love and walked the path of suffering, not out of fear but out of compassion. Your yes at every step of the journey opened the door to my redemption. You are the obedient Son—and because of You, I am no longer condemned.

Thank You for surrendering fully to the cross. Thank You for staying the course when everything in You cried out for relief. You endured for the joy set before You—and I am part of that joy. I receive the power of Your obedience in my life today. I am justified. I am made right. I am forever loved. Let that reality rise like leaven in my soul, transforming how I think, how I respond, and how I live. Amen.

5

HE ENDURED THE CROSS FOR YOUR JOY

Hebrews 12:2 (NIV) For the joy set before him he endured the cross, scorning its shame, and sat down at the right hand of the throne of God.

The cross wasn't a moment of triumph in the eyes of the world—it was torture. It was shame, blood, sweat, and suffocating agony. Yet Jesus endured it—not with dread, but with joy burning in His heart. What kind of joy can sustain someone through that kind of suffering? Only one: the joy of seeing you redeemed.

The joy set before Him wasn't comfort, applause, or even just the resurrection. It was you. You were the joy. The thought of you forgiven, whole, filled with the Spirit, reunited with the Father—that was the reward He fixed His eyes on. And for that joy, He stayed on the path of suffering. He faced the cruelty of man, the silence of heaven, the torment of sin's full weight—and He kept going.

Isaiah 53:11 (NKJV) says, "He shall see the labor of His soul, and be satisfied." That means when Jesus looked ahead to what His suffering would produce, He said, "It's worth it." You were worth it. The cross wasn't meaningless pain—it was a love-soaked mission. A redemption plan measured not in blood alone, but in joy. He scorned the shame, not because it wasn't real, but because the value of your life outweighed the disgrace of the cross.

He was abandoned so you could be brought close. He was stripped of dignity so you could wear His righteousness. He tasted death so you could live forever. There was nothing random about His suffering—every moment was loaded with purpose. Every step toward the cross was a declaration: *You matter. You're worth saving. I'll endure anything to bring you home.*

Now He is seated at the right hand of the throne of God, not just as the crucified Lamb, but as the victorious King. And you are part of His joy—His inheritance, His delight, His reward. That means your value isn't measured by what you do but by what He was willing to do for you.

Affirmation: Jesus wasn't forced to die—He chose the cross because He chose me. Love held Him there. I am deeply valued and eternally loved by the One who gave His life for mine.

Prayer: Jesus, You saw beyond the cross. You saw me—redeemed, forgiven, whole—and You considered that joy greater than the agony. Thank You for enduring every blow, every insult, every nail. You scorned the shame because You saw the outcome. You saw my freedom, and You never turned away.

Let Your love become my confidence. Let the weight of what You endured reveal the depth of what I'm worth to You—not because of anything I've done, but because You chose me. You finished Your work, and now You're seated in victory. That same joy that led You to the cross now fills my heart. It softens my fear, silences my shame, and lifts my eyes to the Father.

You didn't regret the cross. You called it joy. Let that love rise in me like leaven—quietly shaping every part of me until I live with the same joy You died to give. Amen.

6

HE BECAME SIN SO I COULD BECOME RIGHTEOUS

2 Corinthians 5:21 (NKJV) For He made Him who knew no sin to be sin for us, that we might become the righteousness of God in Him.

Jesus didn't simply carry sin like a burden strapped to His back—He became it. The sinless One—the Lamb without blemish—was made sin. Every vile thought, hidden shame, selfish act, and generational curse—He absorbed them into Himself. On the cross, Jesus became the embodiment of all that was wrong so you could become everything that is right.

This is the divine exchange at the center of the gospel: He became what we were so we could become what He is. He stood in our place as the guilty, so we could stand in His place as the blameless. Not just pardoned, but righteous. Not just forgiven, but clean. This righteousness isn't achieved through effort—it's received by faith. It's not a status we maintain by performance but a gift we inherit by grace.

Romans 3:22 (NLT) says, "We are made right with God by placing our faith in Jesus Christ. And this is true for everyone who believes, no matter who we are." Your past doesn't disqualify you. Your struggle doesn't define you. In Christ, you are the righteousness of God—not someday, but right now. You are no longer sin-conscious; you are righteousness-conscious. That means you can come boldly to the Father without fear, without shame, without trying to earn what's already been given.

You are not just "trying to be better." You have been made new. The old is gone. The sin that once identified you was crucified with Christ, and now His identity defines you. He became sin once, so you would never again be identified by it. His work is finished. Your identity is secure.

Let this truth rise inside you: you are righteous. Not by works, but by blood. Not by striving, but by union. Let it silence the voice of shame and calm the fear of judgment. Let it reshape how you pray, how you think, and how you live.

Affirmation: Jesus became what I was—sin—so I could become what He is—righteous. I don't have to earn righteousness; I receive it as a gift. I am clean, accepted, and justified in Him.

Prayer: Jesus, You became sin for me. You took what I was so I could become what You are—righteous, pure, and wholly accepted by the Father. You didn't just deal with my sin—you exchanged it for Your holiness. Thank You for the scandalous beauty of this grace. I don't deserve it, but You gave it freely.

Let Your righteousness settle in my heart today. Let it wash away every trace of shame, guilt, or insecurity. I stand in Your victory. I live from Your finished work. I am righteous in You—not someday, but now. Let this truth rise like leaven within me, renewing my mind, healing my soul, and shaping how I see myself forever. Amen.

7

HE BECAME THE CURSE TO REDEEM ME

Galatians 3:13 (NKJV) Christ has redeemed us from the curse of the law, having become a curse for us (for it is written, "Cursed is everyone who hangs on a tree").

Sin didn't just bring guilt—it brought a curse. Under the law, every failure, every missed commandment, every disobedient act carried consequences. And those consequences were heavy: shame, separation, sickness, fear, and ultimately death. The law demanded perfection, and anything less brought a curse. But in love, Jesus did what we could never do. He fulfilled the law perfectly—then took our failure as His own. He became the curse so you could go free.

On the cross, Jesus didn't just carry your sin—He absorbed the full curse that sin produced. Every consequence of disobedience listed in Deuteronomy 28—poverty, confusion, oppression, weakness, fear—was aimed at Him. He took it all willingly so that none of it would have a legal right to remain in your life. The curse was transferred to Him, and His blessing was transferred to you.

Colossians 2:14 (CSB) says, "He erased the certificate of debt, with its obligations, that was against us and opposed to us, and has taken it away by nailing it to the cross." That means every record of failure, every accusation the enemy could use against you, every generational pattern tied to sin and brokenness—it was nailed to the cross and left there. Jesus didn't just tear up your debt; He destroyed the system that kept you bound to it.

You are not cursed. You are not condemned. You are not disqualified by your past or bound by your bloodline. You are redeemed. The curse has been broken at the root, and the blessing of Christ has been planted in its place. Galatians 3:14 continues, saying that the blessing of Abraham now comes upon the Gentiles in Christ. That means everything God promised—righteousness, provision, peace, and purpose—is now your inheritance.

Let this truth saturate your soul: Jesus became the curse so you could live under the blessing. His cross wasn't just forgiveness—it was freedom. His sacrifice didn't just wash away guilt—it severed every tie to judgment.

Affirmation: Jesus bore every curse that belonged to me so I could inherit every blessing that belongs to Him. I no longer live under judgment—I live under divine favor.

Prayer: Jesus, thank You for becoming the curse in my place. You took what I deserved—every consequence of sin, every accusation of the law—and You bore it fully. You hung on the tree, not for Your failure, but for mine. And in doing so, You redeemed me completely. No curse has a right to linger in my life.

You nailed my condemnation to the cross. You erased the record that stood against me. And now I stand in Your righteousness, surrounded by Your blessing. I am free. I am clean. I am redeemed. Let this truth echo through every corner of my heart. Let it uproot fear, silence accusation, and empower me to live boldly in Your finished work.

8

HE NAILED THE LAW'S ACCUSATION AGAINST ME TO THE CROSS

Colossians 2:14 (NLT) He canceled the record of the charges against us and took it away by nailing it to the cross.

The law didn't just expose sin—it documented it. Like a courtroom transcript, it kept a record of every infraction, every misstep, every failure to measure up. It was a list that stood against us, demanding justice, and it gave the accuser ammunition to heap shame and fear on our hearts. But Jesus didn't just cover that list—He destroyed it. On the cross, He took the full record and drove nails through it with His own hands.

This wasn't a metaphor. It was a legal act. A heavenly transaction. The charges against you—past, present, and future—were taken away entirely. Paid in full. Canceled forever. The scroll of your guilt didn't just disappear—it was executed on the cross. That means there is *nothing* left to accuse you. No sin that still hangs over your head. No secret that still has power to shame you. No failure that defines you.

Romans 8:1 (NKJV) says, "There is therefore now no condemnation to those who are in Christ Jesus." That "now" means this very moment. Not someday when you get your act together. Not after enough time has passed to prove you've changed. Now. You are not condemned. You are not under review. Your case is closed. And the verdict is freedom.

God isn't keeping tabs on your mistakes. The Judge Himself—righteous, holy, and just—has declared you not guilty. And more than that, your file has been shredded. Your history isn't being managed—it's been removed. There's nothing left to separate you from the love of God. There's nothing left to earn.

So when the enemy whispers accusation, point to the cross. When your own heart replays your worst moments, point to the cross. When shame creeps in like a familiar shadow, point to the cross. That's where your record went—and it's never coming back.

Affirmation: Jesus didn't just become my sin—He became my sorrow, my grief, and my heartbreak. I can bring every pain to Him and find comfort, healing, and peace in His embrace.

Prayer: Jesus, thank You for nailing every accusation to the cross. You didn't just forgive me—you removed the entire record. Every charge. Every shameful moment. Every reason for guilt. You took it all, and You silenced the accuser with Your blood.

I don't have to live under condemnation. I am not on trial. I am declared righteous, washed clean, and forever accepted in You. Let that truth echo louder than every lie. Let it rebuild my confidence and restore my joy. You are not keeping score—I am free.

Let this truth rise in me like leaven—displacing shame, destroying fear, and releasing me into the fullness of grace. Amen.

9

HE BORE MY SICKNESS AND DISEASE SO I CAN BE HEALED

Isaiah 53:4 (NKJV) Surely He has borne our griefs and carried our sorrows; yet we esteemed Him stricken, smitten by God, and afflicted.

The cross was not only about sin—it was about suffering. Jesus didn't just take on our guilt; He stepped into our pain. The Hebrew words used in Isaiah 53:4 are rich with meaning. "Griefs" points to sickness, weakness, and even mental or emotional affliction. "Sorrows" refers to anguish, deep pain, and trauma. Jesus didn't turn away from our darkest moments—He took them upon Himself.

He bore the weight of every loss, every heartbreak, every silent cry. He didn't ignore our suffering or leave it out of His redemptive work. He embraced it fully. The betrayals we've endured, the people we've lost, the moments of crushing disappointment—Jesus carried them. He entered the deepest places of human sorrow so that no pain would ever be too dark for His light or too heavy for His shoulders.

Psalm 147:3 says, "He heals the brokenhearted and binds up their wounds." That isn't poetic wishful thinking—it's the result of the cross. The healing didn't start with your recovery; it started with His suffering. On the cross, Jesus became acquainted with grief so you could be made whole. He wrapped Himself in your sorrow so He could clothe you with comfort.

You are not alone in your pain. Jesus doesn't meet you at a distance—He meets you in the midst. He understands the weight you carry, and He offers to lift it. His empathy isn't theoretical; it's experiential. He wept. He grieved. He anguished. And He did it not just for sympathy—but for healing.

Let this truth find its way deep into your soul: Jesus carried what you were never meant to hold forever. And now, because of Him, restoration is not just possible—it's promised.

Affirmation: Every wound Jesus bore was for my wholeness. By His stripes, I am healed—physically, emotionally, and spiritually. Healing is mine because of Him.

Prayer: Jesus, You carried what crushed me. You didn't ignore my grief—you bore it. You didn't turn away from my sorrow—you entered into it. Thank You for loving me with such compassion that You chose to carry not only my sin, but my heartbreak. Thank You for taking on every tear, every ache, every unspoken wound.

Heal the places that still hurt. Speak peace into the pain I've hidden. Fill the hollow spaces with Your presence and restore what's been broken. I trust You with my sorrow. I give You the grief I've carried for too long. Thank You for walking with me through the valley and never letting go.

Let this truth rise like leaven—gentle, steady, healing. Let it transform my pain into peace and remind me that I am never alone. Amen.

10

HE WAS PUNISHED FOR MY PEACE

Isaiah 53:5 (NIV) But he was pierced for our transgressions, he was crushed for our iniquities; the punishment that brought us peace was on him, and by his wounds we are healed.

Sin isn't just a concept—it's a wound in the fabric of our lives and relationships. Transgressions are our deliberate acts of rebellion, and iniquities are the twisted tendencies that live deep within us. Both cry out for justice, and both carry consequences. But Jesus didn't ask us to bear them. He stepped into the judgment that should have been ours and bore it in His own body.

He was pierced where we deserved to be pierced—wounded by nails, thorns, and spear. He was crushed by the weight of our guilt, grief, and corruption. He didn't just suffer physically. He suffered emotionally, spiritually, cosmically—for you. His soul bore the pressure of divine justice, and in that agony, He secured your peace.

Romans 4:25 (CSB) says, "He was delivered up for our trespasses and raised for our justification." That means the cross wasn't the end of your story—it was the beginning of your freedom. Jesus was handed over because of your sin, and He was raised because you've been made right. There is no wrath left for you. There is no penalty hanging over your head. Everything that separated you from God was removed at the cross.

His punishment became your peace. His wounds became your healing. You don't have to fear judgment or anticipate rejection. You are no longer under the weight of sin's demand. Jesus carried it, satisfied it, and declared it finished. Now peace is your portion, and healing is your right.

This is personal. He didn't just die for sin in general—He died for your sin. Your worst moments. Your hidden shame. Your longings to be free. He was pierced so you wouldn't have to carry the sting. He was crushed so you wouldn't have to be shattered. And what He gave in return is more than forgiveness—it's wholeness.

Affirmation: Jesus took the punishment I deserved so I could have the peace He lived in. I don't have to live anxious or afraid—His peace guards my heart and mind.

Prayer: Jesus, You were pierced for me. Every act of rebellion, every broken piece of my heart, every twisted part of my past—you bore it all. You didn't turn away from my sin. You took it into Yourself. Thank You for enduring the punishment that brought me peace. Thank You for the healing that flows from Your wounds.

I receive that peace today. I receive healing in every place where pain has lived too long. You paid the price in full. There's nothing left for me to earn. Nothing left to fear. I rest in what You've finished. I rejoice in the peace You bought for me. Let Your love mend what's been broken.

11

HE WAS CRUSHED FOR MY INIQUITIES

Isaiah 53:5 (NKJV) But He was wounded for our transgressions, He was bruised for our iniquities; the chastisement for our peace was upon Him, and by His stripes we are healed.

Not all pain is visible. Not all sin is obvious. Iniquity is the deep-down distortion sin causes—the inner twisting of the soul that shapes how we think, feel, and see ourselves. It's the inherited brokenness, the shame that clings, the patterns we can't seem to shake. It's not just what we do wrong—it's what's been wrong inside us. And Jesus didn't just come to fix our behavior. He came to heal the root.

Isaiah says He was "bruised" or "crushed" for our iniquities. That word points to internal injury—pain beneath the surface, wounds no one else sees. Jesus was crushed emotionally, mentally, spiritually—His soul overwhelmed in Gethsemane, His body broken at Calvary. He bore the full weight of the damage sin does on the inside. He took the twisted, shame-filled places we try to hide, and He took them into Himself.

This wasn't a superficial rescue. Jesus didn't just clean up the outside—He went into the depths of human brokenness. Every secret ache, every distorted desire, every deep place that feels "too much" or "too far gone"—He went there. And He didn't recoil. He embraced it, bore it, and broke its power.

Hebrews 10:10 (CSB) says, "We have been sanctified through the offering of the body of Jesus Christ once for all time." That word "sanctified" means made whole, made holy, made clean. Once. For all. You are not a work-in-progress trying to become worthy—you are someone Jesus declared whole when He offered Himself in your place.

So don't be afraid of what's under the surface. Don't hide the parts of you that still feel broken. He already took them. His bruises are proof. He was crushed so you wouldn't have to live crushed. His offering went deeper than your dysfunction and pulled healing into places you didn't even know needed it.

Affirmation: Jesus was abandoned and rejected so I could be welcomed and embraced. I am no longer trying to earn approval—I am fully accepted by God.

Prayer: Jesus, You were crushed for my iniquities. Not just my choices, but the places in me that feel twisted, wounded, and beyond repair. You didn't avoid the mess inside me—you entered it. You bore my inward pain and offered healing in return. Thank You for going deeper than I even realized I needed. You didn't just die for what I did—you died for what sin did to me.

I invite Your presence into every hidden place. Into the shame I still carry, the patterns I haven't been able to break, the wounds I struggle to name. Touch the roots. Restore the places that feel warped. You were bruised for these very things. You make me whole from the inside out.

Let this truth rise like leaven—quietly, powerfully, deeply—until it reshapes my self-image, my emotions, my identity, and my hope. You were crushed so I could be made whole. And I receive that wholeness now. Amen.

12

THE PUNISHMENT THAT BROUGHT ME PEACE WITH GOD WAS UPON HIM

Isaiah 53:5 (NIV) ...the punishment that brought us peace was on him, and by his wounds we are healed.

Peace isn't just silence or a break from stress. True peace—*shalom* in Hebrew—is far more. It means wholeness, well-being, safety, harmony, friendship with God, and prosperity in the deepest sense. And this peace didn't come cheaply. Jesus didn't just calm the storm around us—He absorbed the storm of judgment that was meant for us.

The punishment that brought us peace was no mild sentence. It was the full force of divine justice falling on Jesus. He bore the wrath, the separation, the agony that sin required—not because He deserved it, but because He wanted you to live in the peace He's always known with the Father.

Romans 5:1 (NKJV) says, "Therefore, having been justified by faith, we have peace with God through our Lord Jesus Christ." Justified means declared righteous—fully and permanently—and that declaration is the doorway to peace. You are not under condemnation. You are not on probation. You're not being tolerated by God; you are at peace with Him.

Jesus took the punishment so there would be nothing left between you and the Father. No shame. No striving. No fear. That means your relationship with God isn't fragile—it's secure. Peace isn't a feeling you chase. It's a position you've been given. Jesus earned it. And He gave it to you.

That peace is more than a theological idea—it's a living force within you. Philippians 4:7 calls it "the peace of God, which surpasses all understanding," and says it will guard your heart and mind. It's peace that doesn't make sense to the world. Peace that steadies you when circumstances shake. Peace that anchors you in the love of a God who already declared you righteous.

Let this truth wash over you: Jesus was punished so you could be whole. You're not striving for peace. You're living in the overflow of His obedience.

Affirmation: Jesus stayed silent in the face of injustice so I could always have a voice before the Father. My prayers matter. Heaven hears me.

Prayer: Jesus, You took the punishment I deserved so I could have the peace You've always known. You bore the wrath, the judgment, and the weight of sin's penalty so I could stand in the Father's presence without fear. Thank You for paying the full price for my peace.

Let that peace guard my heart today. Let it still the storms inside me. Let it push back every anxious thought, every lie that says I'm not enough, every fear that whispers I'm still far away. I rest in Your finished work. I receive Your eternal *shalom*—peace with God, peace in my soul, peace that surpasses understanding.

Let this peace rise like leaven—filling every part of me, making me whole from the inside out. Amen.

13

BY HIS STRIPES I AM HEALED

Isaiah 53:5 (NKJV) ...and by His stripes we are healed.

The lashes Jesus endured were not meaningless cruelty. They were purpose-driven, power-filled, and eternally effective. Each stripe torn into His flesh was a blow against the kingdom of darkness—against sickness, disease, pain, and every kind of brokenness. His wounds weren't accidental—they were intentional, taken in your place so you could walk in wholeness.

Healing isn't an afterthought in the gospel—it's woven into the sacrifice itself. Isaiah prophesied it, and 1 Peter 2:24 confirms it: "By His stripes you were healed." That's past tense. It's already done. Healing isn't something you earn through perfect faith or good behavior—it's part of your inheritance as a child of God. Jesus bore your sickness just as surely as He bore your sin.

Whether your need is physical, emotional, or mental—Jesus has already made provision. The same cross that secured your forgiveness also secured your healing. And while we may not always understand the timing or the process, the promise remains unchanged: healing has been paid for in full.

He didn't just carry sin—He carried pain. Isaiah 53:4 says He "carried our sorrows," and Matthew 8:17 echoes it: "He Himself took our infirmities and bore our sicknesses." There is no part of human suffering that Jesus did not step into. And because He bore it, you can boldly receive what He purchased—wholeness, restoration, and health.

This doesn't mean we pretend pain doesn't exist. It means we anchor our hope in the finished work of Jesus. We pray, we believe, we speak life—and we rest in the knowledge that our healing was secured at the cross. The stripes on His back testify to your freedom from affliction.

Let this truth settle deep in your heart: Healing is not something you beg for—it's something you receive. Jesus made the down payment with His own blood.

Affirmation: Though sinless, Jesus was numbered among sinners so I could be counted among the righteous. I am no longer defined by my past but by His perfection.

Prayer: Jesus, thank You for every stripe You endured. You didn't suffer for nothing. You took my sickness, my pain, and my weakness into Your own body. Each wound on Your back shouted, "Healed. Whole. Free." I receive what You paid for. I speak life over every cell in my body, every burden in my heart, every wound in my soul.

You are my healer. You are faithful. And I trust You—not just with my salvation, but with my healing. Let Your wholeness flow through me today. I rest in what You've already accomplished.

Let Your healing rise like leaven—quietly but powerfully—through every part of me, until no brokenness remains untouched by Your love. Amen.

14

HE WAS OPPRESSED AND AFFLICTED FOR MY FREEDOM

Isaiah 53:7 (NKJV) He was oppressed and He was afflicted, yet He opened not His mouth; He was led as a lamb to the slaughter, and as a sheep before its shearers is silent, so He opened not His mouth.

When Jesus stood before His accusers, He had every right to speak. Every right to call down angels, defend His innocence, or silence the injustice surrounding Him. But He didn't. He remained silent—not out of weakness, but out of strength. He bore the full weight of oppression and affliction so that you would never have to carry it alone—or forever.

Oppression and affliction describe pressure from every side—emotional, spiritual, physical. Jesus felt the crushing weight of false accusation, cruel abuse, spiritual darkness, and bodily torment. He was boxed in, rejected, misunderstood, and mistreated. And yet, He did not open His mouth. Not because He was powerless—but because He was purposeful.

His silence wasn't surrender to injustice—it was surrender to love. He didn't defend Himself, because He was defending *you*. He absorbed the wrath of man and the curse of sin, offering no resistance, so that nothing could ever stand between you and freedom again.

Galatians 5:1 (NLT) says, "So Christ has truly set us free. Now make sure that you stay free…" His freedom wasn't just a theological concept—it was bought through silent, sacred suffering. He let Himself be bound so your chains could break. He endured injustice so you could walk in the justice of God. His voice was quiet so yours could be bold with truth, joy, and praise.

You are not bound. You are not forgotten. You are not under the weight of oppression anymore. You are free—fully and forever. You may still face pressure, but it cannot define you. You may still hear the whispers of condemnation, but they have no authority. Jesus' silence shouted your victory through eternity. His affliction birthed your liberation.

Affirmation: Jesus bore oppression so I could live free. No chain, no stronghold, no lie has power over me anymore. I am free indeed.

Prayer: Jesus, You were oppressed so I could be free. You were afflicted so I could live whole. Thank You for staying silent when injustice surrounded You. Thank You for choosing surrender, not because You were weak, but because You were fighting for me. I honor that holy silence. I receive the freedom You purchased through it.

Let that freedom rise in me today. Break every invisible chain. Lift every lingering burden. Let Your peace flood my soul and give me a voice of victory. I am no longer bound—I am beloved, chosen, and free in You.

Let this truth rise like leaven—subtle, powerful, unstoppable—until it changes how I see myself and how I live. Amen.

15

HE WAS JUDGED GUILTY SO I COULD BE JUSTIFIED

Isaiah 53:8 (NKJV) He was taken from prison and from judgment, and who will declare His generation? For He was cut off from the land of the living; for the transgressions of My people He was stricken.

Jesus didn't face justice—He faced judgment. Pulled from prison in the dark of night, tried in secret, and condemned by those who should have recognized Him, He stood before rulers who mocked the very truth they were witnessing. But far beyond the human injustice was the weight of divine judgment. Not for His sins, but for ours.

He was cut off so we could be brought in. He was stricken so we could be spared. He bore not only the abuse of man but the sentence of heaven, absorbing the penalty that stood between us and God. The judgment we feared—the separation we deserved—was placed entirely on Him.

Romans 3:24 (NLT) says, "Yet God, in His grace, freely makes us right in His sight. He did this through Christ Jesus when He freed us from the penalty for our sins." That's what justification means: not just forgiveness, but full acquittal. A verdict of *righteous* declared over your life by the Judge of the universe.

There is no unfinished sentence hanging over you. No legal claim left unresolved. In Jesus, the gavel has already come down—not with condemnation, but with grace. He took your guilt and gave you His innocence. You don't stand in the court of Heaven awaiting a decision. You stand in Christ, already justified.

So when you feel accused, remember: Jesus already stood in your place. When shame rises, remember: He was cut off so you never would be. When doubt creeps in, return to the cross—where judgment fell once and for all, and justification rose in its place.

Let this truth take root in your soul: You are not on trial. You are not half-accepted. You are fully, freely, forever justified.

Affirmation: Jesus endured unjust judgment so I could stand justified before God. I don't have to fear condemnation—I am declared righteous by the Judge of all.

Prayer: Jesus, You were judged as me, now I don't have to fear judgment. You were condemned so I could be declared righteous. Thank You for taking the sentence that should have fallen on me. Thank You for being cut off so I could be brought close. You stood silent beneath the gavel, not because You were guilty, but because You were bearing my guilt.

Now I stand in Your righteousness. I am justified. I am clean. I am whole. I choose to let that truth reshape how I see myself. I allow it to silence every accusation and restore every place shame tried to settle. I am not condemned—I am declared right in Your sight.

16

HE WAS CUT OFF SO I COULD BE BROUGHT NEAR

Ephesians 2:13 (CSB) But now in Christ Jesus, you who were far away have been brought near by the blood of Christ.

Separation was the price of sin. From the garden of Eden to the veil in the temple, humanity's fall created a painful distance between God and His people. But Jesus came to close that gap. And the way He did it was not by avoiding the pain of separation—but by walking straight into it. He was cut off—exiled from safety, stripped of connection, and even forsaken in His final moments—not for His guilt, but for yours.

Isaiah 53:8 says He was "cut off from the land of the living," an image of isolation, finality, and judgment. He bore the full weight of what it means to be separated, not just physically but spiritually. That moment on the cross when He cried out to the Father and received no answer—it was the price of our proximity. He endured distance so we could be brought near.

Ephesians 2:13 makes it personal: *you* who were far away. Whether the distance came from shame, rebellion, confusion, or pain—it's been erased. The blood of Christ didn't just forgive your sin, it tore down every wall between you and God. You're not outside. You're not on probation. You're not being held at arm's length. You've been brought *all the way in*.

Hebrews 10:22 reminds us to "draw near with a true heart in full assurance of faith." That means nearness is not a goal—it's your starting place. You're not working to get closer to God; you're walking from the nearness Jesus already secured. You're not climbing toward His presence—you're already there.

This changes everything. You can speak boldly. Worship freely. Rest deeply. You are no longer far— you are home. Jesus didn't just remove the barrier— He became the way. Now, because He was cut off, you will never be.

Affirmation: Jesus was cut off from life so I could be brought near to God. I'm no longer on the outside —I belong in His presence, close to His heart.

Prayer: Jesus, You were cut off so I could be brought near. You were cast out so I could be brought in. Thank You for stepping into the loneliness and judgment that I deserved. You didn't flinch from separation—you bore it fully to bring me close forever.

Now I live in the reality of Your nearness. No veil. No shame. No striving. Let that truth echo in my soul today. Let it reshape how I relate to You—with confidence, not hesitation. With boldness, not fear. I rest in Your closeness. I live from Your love.

Let this truth rise like leaven in my soul—removing every lie of distance, softening every place that still feels far, and pulling my heart deeper into the reality of Your embrace. Amen.

17

HE WAS BURIED IN A RICH MAN'S TOMB TO FULFILL THE WORD

Isaiah 53:9 (NIV) He was assigned a grave with the wicked, and with the rich in his death, though he had done no violence, nor was any deceit in his mouth.

Jesus died the death of a criminal, crucified between thieves, condemned by the world. Yet in a surprising twist, He was buried in the tomb of a wealthy man. Joseph of Arimathea—a member of the Jewish council, rich, respected, and secretly a disciple—offered his own new tomb for Jesus' body. It was an act of reverence, honor, and courage. But more than that, it was the precise fulfillment of prophecy.

Isaiah had written centuries earlier that the Messiah would be "assigned a grave with the wicked, and with the rich in his death." That contrast seemed impossible—how could He be buried with both? And yet, Jesus died among the guilty and was buried among the elite. The Scripture was fulfilled down to the smallest detail.

Matthew 27:57–60 records this exact moment. A rich man steps forward, and the Word unfolds with precision. This wasn't coincidence or convenience — it was divine orchestration. Even in death, Jesus' story followed the script written long before. Nothing was out of place. Nothing was random. God's Word held true, even in the darkness of the grave.

Why does this matter to you? Because it reveals the meticulous faithfulness of God. If He ensured that even Jesus' burial fulfilled prophecy, He will fulfill every promise He has made to you. Your salvation isn't accidental. Your redemption isn't loosely held together. It is secure, crafted, and foretold by a God who watches over His Word to perform it.

Every thread in Jesus' story — every moment, every movement, every promise — was woven together with purpose. And the same God who carried out that plan with precision is the One who holds your life now. He finishes what He starts. He fulfills what He speaks.

Let this truth anchor your soul: if God honored every line of prophecy in Jesus' death and burial, He will honor every promise He's made to you in Christ.

Affirmation: Jesus fulfilled every prophecy, down to the details of His burial. His faithfulness to the Word gives me confidence that God keeps every promise.

Prayer: Father, thank You for the assurance that Your Word never fails. You fulfilled every detail of Jesus' life, death, and burial—not one prophecy fell short. Thank You for showing me that nothing is accidental in Your plan. I trust that what You began in Christ, You will complete in me.

Let this truth build confidence in my heart today. You are a finisher. You are faithful in the smallest details. I rest in Your perfect plan. Let my faith be rooted in Your Word and rise strong in the assurance that You will do what You have said.

Let that faith rise like leaven in my soul—quietly but powerfully—until it shapes every expectation I carry. Amen.

18

HE DESCENDED INTO HADES SO I'D NEVER BE FORSAKEN

Ephesians 4:9 (NKJV) Now this, "He ascended" — what does it mean but that He also first descended into the lower parts of the earth?

Psalm 139:8 (NKJV) If I ascend into heaven, You are there; if I make my bed in hell, behold, You are there.

When Jesus died, His body lay in the tomb, but His spirit descended into the depths—into the realm of the dead. He went to the lowest place a soul could reach. Why? So no part of creation, no dimension of suffering, no corner of darkness would be untouched by His victory. He went there willingly so you'd never have to.

Sin brought separation—true separation from God, from life, from peace. But Jesus bore that separation in full. He entered the grave, suffered your separation, and rose as a conqueror. His descent was not the end—it was the beginning of resurrection. His humility wasn't weakness—it was love in its deepest form. He didn't avoid the darkness; He walked straight into it and lit it up with redemption.

Acts 2:27 (CSB) echoes David's prophetic words about the Messiah: "Because you will not abandon me in Hades or allow your holy one to see decay." Jesus trusted the Father even in death. And God did not leave Him there. He raised Him up—and in doing so, raised us too. You are now joined to the risen Christ. His descent secured your resurrection.

This means there is no valley you walk through alone. No depression, no grief, no moment of despair is untouched by His presence. He's already been to the lowest place, and He filled it with Himself. He knows what it's like to be cut off, silenced, and surrounded by darkness. And He broke it open from the inside.

So now, even your lowest place is not forsaken ground. It's redeemed ground. He is with you—always. He went where you could not go, so that in Him, you would never be abandoned again.

Affirmation: Jesus went to the lowest depths so I would never be abandoned. No matter how dark it gets, I am never alone—He is with me always.

Prayer: Jesus, You descended so I would never be alone. You went into death, into the silence, into separation—so that no darkness could ever claim me. You bore the ultimate loneliness so I could live forever connected to the Father. Thank You for filling every valley with Your presence. Thank You for turning graves into gateways.

Even in my lowest moment, You are there. Even when I feel forgotten, You remind me that I'm held. Let Your victory echo in every place of despair. Let Your light break into every shadow. You are my life, my rescue, and my constant companion.

Let this truth rise like leaven in my soul—expanding hope, quieting fear, and anchoring me in the truth that I will never be forsaken. Amen.

19

HE WAS RAISED FROM THE DEAD BECAUSE HE REMAINED FAITHFUL

Acts 2:24 (ESV) God raised him up, loosing the pangs of death, because it was not possible for him to be held by it.

Romans 6:9 (CSB) Because we know that Christ, having been raised from the dead, will not die again. Death no longer rules over him.

Jesus didn't face death because He deserved it—He faced it because He was faithful. He obeyed the Father fully, all the way to His final breath and into the grave. He endured betrayal, false accusation, torture, and crucifixion without ever sinning, complaining, or turning back. He remained faithful even unto death and descent into Hades.

Acts 2:24 declares that "it was not possible for Him to be held" by death. Why? Because the grave has no hold on holiness. Jesus was the spotless Lamb, the perfect Son, the obedient Servant. He fulfilled the law, absorbed the wrath, and broke the curse. And when the work was finished, God raised Him—not just to prove His divinity, but to proclaim His victory.

Romans 6:9 tells us that Jesus can never die again. Death no longer rules over Him—and if you are in Him, it no longer rules over you either. His resurrection wasn't just the end of His suffering—it was the beginning of your new life. It was the inauguration of eternal victory. It means fear has lost its grip. Shame has lost its voice. Death has lost its sting.

Romans 8:11 says the same Spirit who raised Jesus from the dead now lives in you. That's not just comfort—it's empowerment. The Spirit that conquered the grave is actively working in your heart, mind, and body to bring renewal, healing, and strength. Resurrection life isn't reserved for the future—it begins now.

You are no longer defined by death. You're not under the rule of failure or fear. Jesus' faithfulness unlocked resurrection power, and now that same power lives in you. You rise because He rose. You live because He lives. The tomb is empty, and because of that, your heart can be full.

Affirmation: Jesus was raised in glory because He remained faithful through death. That same power now lives in me, bringing resurrection life to my spirit every day.

Prayer: Father, thank You for raising Jesus in power. He remained faithful, obedient, and pure—and You did not leave Him in the grave. Because of His faithfulness, I now live in the power of resurrection. Thank You that death could not hold Him, and in Him, it cannot hold me either.

Let resurrection life flood every place in me that still feels lifeless or weighed down. Let the same Spirit that raised Christ quicken my body, renew my thinking, and stir my spirit. I receive Your life, Your power, and Your victory today. Jesus, You are alive —and so am I in You.

Let this truth rise in me, resurrecting hope, reviving purpose, and reminding me that the grave has no power over me. Amen.

20

HE OVERCAME THE POWER OF DEATH

Hebrews 2:14 (NLT) Because God's children are human beings—made of flesh and blood—the Son also became flesh and blood. For only as a human being could he die, and only by dying could he break the power of the devil, who had the power of death.

Death once ruled as humanity's greatest fear—an unavoidable end, a looming separation, a thief of hope. And behind it stood the enemy, wielding the fear of death like a weapon. But Jesus came to destroy that power at its root. He didn't sidestep death. He met it face-to-face. As one of us, in flesh and blood, He walked right into the grave—and broke it open from the inside.

Only as a human could He die, and only through death could He break the devil's grip. The cross was not a defeat—it was a divine strategy. Through His suffering and surrender, Jesus stripped death of its finality and crushed the fear that enslaved us. Revelation 1:18 declares that He holds the keys of death and Hades. That means the enemy doesn't even have the keys to his own domain anymore.

Jesus holds them. Keys represent authority and He has it ALL!

Death has been declawed. Its sting is gone. Its grip is shattered. And in Christ, you are no longer subject to it—not just in eternity, but now. The fear of death, the anxiety about your future, the torment of what-ifs and unknowns—all of it has been overcome. You live in the shadow of a resurrected King, not a threatening grave.

Eternal life doesn't begin when you die—it began the moment you believed. You have already passed from death into life (John 5:24). The resurrection power that raised Jesus from the dead is alive in you right now. And nothing—not even death—can separate you from the love of God in Christ.

Let this truth flood your soul: Jesus didn't just beat death for Himself—He beat it for you. You are free from the fear of it. You are anchored in eternal life. You are held by the One who holds the keys.

Affirmation: Jesus didn't just die—He defeated death. Because He lives, I live. Death has no sting and no victory over me anymore.

Prayer:
Jesus, You overcame death—not just for Yourself, but for me. You broke its power, silenced its threats,

and reclaimed the keys from the enemy. I no longer live under the fear of death. I live in the security of Your resurrection.

Thank You for facing what I couldn't face and winning the battle I could never fight. You are my confidence, my life, and my eternal hope. Let that victory echo in every part of me today. Fill me with boldness, with peace, with assurance that I am never at the mercy of darkness again.

21

HE ASCENDED WITH HIS OWN BLOOD TO SECURE ETERNAL REDEMPTION

Hebrews 9:12 (NKJV) Not with the blood of goats and calves, but with His own blood He entered the Most Holy Place once for all, having obtained eternal redemption.

The resurrection wasn't the end of Jesus' work—it was the turning point. After rising from the dead, He ascended to the Father. And when He did, He brought His own blood—not in a metaphorical way, but as a real, eternal offering. He entered the heavenly Most Holy Place, not to repeat a ritual, but to seal redemption forever.

Under the Old Covenant, the high priest entered the tabernacle year after year with the blood of animals. It was a cycle—a temporary covering that had to be renewed again and again. But Jesus ended the cycle. As the spotless Lamb and eternal High Priest, He entered once for all time with His own blood. It wasn't just enough—it was more than enough. It didn't delay judgment; it satisfied it.

This changes everything. Your salvation is not seasonal. It's not reset every time you fail. It's not up for renegotiation based on your spiritual performance. It is eternal. The blood of Jesus has already spoken for you in heaven, and that word cannot be reversed. The sacrifice was final, and the result is forever.

Hebrews 10:14 says, "For by one offering He has perfected forever those who are being sanctified." That means your identity is rooted in a finished work, not in an unfinished process. You are being transformed, yes—but you are already redeemed, already accepted, already perfected in Christ.

When doubt rises, look up. When fear whispers that you've gone too far or failed too deeply, remember where the blood is. It's not on an altar built by men. It's in the very presence of God, testifying forever that you belong.

Let this truth take root in your heart: your redemption isn't fragile—it's finished. And your security isn't based on how tightly you're holding on to God, but on how completely He has held on to you in Christ.

Affirmation: Jesus entered heaven as my High Priest, securing my eternal salvation. I am forever redeemed, and nothing can undo His finished work.

Prayer: Jesus, You didn't just shed Your blood—you carried it into heaven for me. You entered the Most Holy Place and secured eternal redemption once for all. Thank You that nothing can reverse what You've done. Thank You that I am not waiting for salvation to last—I am living in a finished covenant that cannot be undone.

Let this truth anchor my heart today. When I feel unsure or unworthy, let me see Your blood in heaven and know I'm accepted, justified, and secure. Let that confidence grow in me until it drives out every trace of fear.

22

HE REMOVED MY SINFUL NATURE AND GAVE ME A NEW HEART

Ezekiel 36:26 (NLT) And I will give you a new heart, and I will put a new spirit in you. I will take out your stony, stubborn heart and give you a tender, responsive heart.

Romans 6:6 (CSB) For we know that our old self was crucified with him so that the body ruled by sin might be rendered powerless, so that we may no longer be enslaved to sin.

Jesus didn't come to improve your old life—He came to crucify it and replace it with something brand new. When you placed your faith in Him, a miracle happened: your old sinful nature—the one bound to sin, resistant to God, and hardened by self—was put to death. You were not patched up. You were made new.

That old self—the one enslaved to sin—was crucified with Christ. And in its place, God gave you a new heart, just as He promised in Ezekiel. A heart that is alive, tender, and responsive. A spirit that desires Him, hears Him, and follows Him. You are no longer spiritually dead—you are born again, recreated from the inside out. You are no longer dead in sin, you are ALIVE in Christ.

Ephesians 4:24 says you were "created according to God, in true righteousness and holiness." That's not your goal—it's your identity. You are not trying to become a new creation. You *are* a new creation. The old has gone, the new has come (2 Corinthians 5:17). You're not dragging your past behind you—you're walking in resurrection life.

This truth changes everything. You're not bound to repeat old patterns or live under the label of who you used to be. Your mind may need renewal, and your habits may need reshaping, but your spirit is already fully transformed. You don't fight for freedom—you live from it. Your identity is not in your struggle, but in your Savior.

Let this truth go deep: You are not who you were. The old self was nailed to the cross and buried. What rose is new, holy, alive, and empowered.

Affirmation: Jesus didn't just cover my sin—He gave me a brand-new heart. I am no longer a slave to sin but alive to God with a heart that hears Him, knows His ways, and naturally obeys His Word.

Prayer: Father, thank You for the miracle of new birth. Thank You that my old self—my sin-bound nature—was crucified with Christ. You didn't leave me in that dead condition. You gave me a new heart and a new spirit. One that is alive to You, sensitive to Your leading, and able to walk in truth.

Help me live from that identity today. Let me see myself the way You see me—whole, clean, and renewed. I choose to reject the lies that say I'm still the same. I choose to walk in the freedom of who I truly am in Christ.

I choose to let this truth transform my thoughts, my emotions, my decisions—as Your Spirit fully aligns with the new heart You've placed within me. Amen.

23

HE UNITED ME WITH GOD BY HIS SPIRIT

1 Corinthians 6:17 (NKJV) But he who is joined to the Lord is one spirit with Him.

Romans 8:9 (NLT) But you are not controlled by your sinful nature. You are controlled by the Spirit if you have the Spirit of God living in you. (And remember that those who do not have the Spirit of Christ living in them do not belong to him at all.)

Salvation is more than being forgiven and rescued from sin—it's being united to God at the deepest level. When you placed your faith in Jesus, something profound happened: the Holy Spirit came to live inside you, and your spirit was fused with His. You didn't just receive forgiveness—you received union. You were joined to the Lord, one spirit with Him.

This isn't poetic metaphor. It's spiritual reality. Galatians 2:20 says, "It is no longer I who live, but Christ lives in me." The same Spirit that raised Jesus from the dead now dwells in you (Romans 8:11). You are not trying to connect with God—you already are. You are not hoping to get closer—He has taken up residence within you.

In the Old Covenant, God's presence dwelled in a physical temple. In the New Covenant, you are that temple. 1 Corinthians 3:16 declares, "Do you not know that you are the temple of God and that the Spirit of God dwells in you?" This means you carry divine presence everywhere you go. You are never alone. Never disconnected. You don't have to conjure God's nearness—His Spirit in you is proof that you're already near.

And because you are joined to Him, your identity has changed. You are not defined by the flesh but led by the Spirit. Romans 8:14 says, "For all who are led by God's Spirit are God's children." You've been grafted into a new family, given a new nature, and empowered by a new source of life. This Spirit-to-spirit union is permanent, personal, and powerful. It's what makes your Christian life possible—not effort, but union. Not striving, but abiding.

You don't pray from a distance. You don't worship hoping He'll show up. You live from the awareness that He's already here. Christ in you is the hope of glory.

Affirmation: I am no longer distant from God. Through Christ and by the Spirit, I am united with Him in deep, unbreakable fellowship.

Prayer: Holy Spirit, thank You for living in me. Thank You for uniting me with Jesus in such a real, permanent, and life-giving way. I'm in awe that I don't have to strive for Your nearness—you've already made me one with You. You've made my heart Your home. You walk with me, speak to me, comfort me, empower me, and guide me from the inside out.

I'm so grateful that I never have to wonder where You are—You're here. You are my constant companion. You have joined Your Spirit with mine so that I can truly know You, walk with You, and become like You. What a gift. What a miracle. What a joy.

Help me live more aware of this union every day. Let it change how I think about myself and how I interact with the world around me. Let it soften me, strengthen me, and remind me who I am—one with Christ, filled with divine life. Let that truth rise in me like leaven until it touches everything I think, say, and do. I am Yours, and You are mine—forever. Amen.

24

HE MADE ME HIS TEMPLE

1 Corinthians 3:16 (CSB) Don't you yourselves know that you are God's temple and that the Spirit of God lives in you?

2 Corinthians 6:16 (NKJV) For you are the temple of the living God. As God has said: "I will dwell in them and walk among them. I will be their God, and they shall be My people."

Under the Old Covenant, God's presence was housed in the innermost room of a man-made temple—the Holy of Holies—separated by a thick veil. Only the high priest could enter, and only once a year, to stand before God on behalf of the people. But when Jesus gave His life on the cross, that veil was torn from top to bottom, declaring that the way to God's presence was now open to all who believe.

Even more astonishing—God didn't just invite you in. He moved in. You became the new temple, the holy dwelling place of the Most High. Not a location, not a ceremony—*you*. The same Spirit who filled the temple with fire and glory now lives in you.

1 Peter 2:5 calls us "living stones" being built into a spiritual house. That means you're not just part of God's family—you're part of His dwelling. You carry His presence with you everywhere you go. Your body, mind, and heart have become sacred ground.

This changes everything. You're not striving to become worthy—His indwelling Spirit has made you holy. You're not hoping for God to come near— He already lives inside you. Your life is no longer ordinary. You are a carrier of divine presence.

And because He lives in you, you bring heaven's influence into every room you enter. Your hands can bring healing. Your words can release peace. Your presence, because of His presence, can shift the atmosphere. You are His temple, and He delights to dwell in you.

I can reveal His presence to every person I encounter. As I am motivated by love for people, I can be His ambassador and minister the very presence of the living God.

Affirmation: I am a dwelling place for God. His Spirit lives in me, and His presence goes with me everywhere I go. I am sacred space.

Prayer: God, I'm honestly in awe that You chose to live in me. Not just visit, not just hover near—but actually make me Your home. You could've picked anywhere in the universe, but You picked me. Not because I'm perfect, but because You love me. That kind of grace undoes me.

Help me remember that everywhere I go, You go too. You're not distant. You're not hard to reach. You're already here—right in the middle of my mess, my thoughts, my day. Let that change how I think, how I speak, how I treat people. Remind me that I carry something holy—not because I'm trying to be spiritual, but because You've made me new.

Thank You for trusting me with Your presence. Thank You for making me Your temple. I don't want to live unaware or distracted. I want to live like it's true—because it is. Let Your Spirit in me overflow into everything I touch today. Amen.

25

HE GAVE ME THE RIGHT TO BE GOD'S CHILD

John 1:12 (NKJV) But as many as received Him, to them He gave the right to become children of God, to those who believe in His name.

Galatians 3:26 (CSB) For through faith you are all sons of God in Christ Jesus.

Jesus didn't just forgive your sins—He gave you a new name, a new family, and a new kind of belonging. When you believed in Him, you weren't just rescued—you were adopted. You were given the legal, eternal right to be God's child. That means your identity isn't up for debate. You're not trying to earn a seat at the table. You were invited, welcomed, and placed in the Father's house with full access to His love.

This is more than spiritual language—it's legal language. You've been given the *right* to be called His child. You're not borrowing a place in the family. You're not a guest. You're not on trial. You are fully, completely, joyfully included. This right is not based on performance. It's rooted in your faith in Jesus and sealed by His blood.

Jesus died not just to deal with sin, but to restore relationship. To open the way for you to live as a son or daughter—not just someday in heaven, but right now. And this sonship comes with all the blessings of family: access, inheritance, intimacy, provision, and security.

Romans 8:15 reminds us, "You did not receive a spirit of slavery to fall back into fear, but you received the Spirit of adoption by whom we cry out, 'Abba, Father!'" This is the cry of someone who knows they are loved. Who knows they're safe. Who knows they belong.

So when fear tries to creep in, or shame tries to disqualify you, or religion tries to make you perform—remember this: You're already in. You already belong. You are a child of God, and that will never change.

Affirmation: I don't just hope I'm a child of God—I know I am. Jesus gave me the right to call God "Father," and nothing can take that away.

Prayer: Father, I can't get over the fact that You call me Your child. Not just someone You rescued, but someone You wanted. Thank You for making me part of Your family—not because I earned it, but because You love me that much. Thank You that I don't have to perform or prove myself—I get to rest in Your love and enjoy being Yours.

Sometimes I forget what that really means. I still act like I have to earn my place. But You remind me that I already belong. I'm already loved. You're not holding anything back from me. You're not ashamed of me. You're proud to call me Yours.

Help me live today like I know I'm Your child. Confident. Secure. At peace. Let Your love shape how I think, how I pray, and how I treat others. Let it calm my fears and quiet the voices of insecurity. You're not just my God—you're my Abba. And I love being Your child. Amen.

26

HE PROMISED ME AN INHERITANCE AS HIS CHILD

Romans 8:17 (NKJV) and if children, then heirs—heirs of God and joint heirs with Christ, if indeed we suffer with Him, that we may also be glorified together.

Ephesians 1:11 (NLT) Furthermore, because we are united with Christ, we have received an inheritance from God, for He chose us in advance, and He makes everything work out according to His plan.

When you trusted in Christ, you didn't just get forgiveness—you stepped into a full inheritance. You became an heir of God and a co-heir with Jesus Himself. That means everything the Father gave to the Son, He shares with you. This isn't a metaphor—it's a spiritual reality with present and eternal implications.

Ephesians 1:3 tells us we've already been blessed with every spiritual blessing in heavenly places. That includes righteousness, peace, joy, healing, wisdom, favor, purpose, and eternal life. And it's not something we earn—it's something we were born into the moment we were born again. You don't have to strive to access God's goodness; you just receive it as a beloved child and rightful heir.

Being an heir means you don't approach life like a beggar or an outsider. You walk in the confidence of someone who knows they belong, someone who has access to heaven's storehouse. Your inheritance isn't just about what happens after you die—it's about living in the fullness of what Jesus paid for now. And yet, there's still more to come. There's a future glory, a perfected world, and a fully restored creation that you are destined to inherit with Christ.

This inheritance shapes everything. It changes how you pray, how you face trials, how you dream. You don't lack. You aren't spiritually poor. You are fully resourced by heaven itself because you belong to God—and He has already given you everything in Christ.

Receive every blessing from your Father who loves you, who took the time to meticulously plan out His last will and testament to leave you an inheritance.

Affirmation: I'm not just saved—I'm an heir. Every spiritual blessing belongs to me in Christ. My future is secure, and my present is full of promise.

Prayer: Father, I'm overwhelmed by what You've given me. I'm not just forgiven—I'm Your heir. You didn't have to do it, but You made me part of Your family and gave me the same inheritance You gave Jesus. That's too big for my mind sometimes, but I choose to believe it. I choose to live from that place of abundance, not from fear or lack.

Help me remember that I'm not scraping by spiritually. You've already given me everything I need. Teach me to walk in what's mine—not with pride, but with confidence rooted in Your love. Remind me that peace, righteousness, healing, and purpose are not things I have to chase—they're already mine in Jesus.

Thank You for choosing me in advance. Thank You for making everything work out according to Your plan. Even when I don't see it, I know You're moving. I trust You with what's mine—not just for the future, but for right now.

27

I AM A JOINT HEIR WITH CHRIST

Romans 8:17 (NIV) Now if we are children, then we are heirs—heirs of God and co-heirs with Christ, if indeed we share in his sufferings in order that we may also share in his glory.

Hebrews 1:1-2 (NASB) God, after He spoke long ago to the fathers in the prophets in many portions and in many ways, in these last days has spoken to us in His Son, whom He appointed heir of all things, through whom He also made the world.

To be a joint heir with Christ means you are not just a recipient of grace—you are a partner in inheritance. Jesus didn't rescue you just to leave you on the sidelines. He brought you all the way into the family and seated you next to God, in Himself. Everything the Father gave to Him—intimacy, access, favor, authority, and glory—He now shares with you. Jesus inherited all things, and He shares everything He is and has with you. God meticulously planned His last will and testament, probated in Christ, and you are included.

This isn't some distant reward that kicks in after you die. It's a present reality rooted in your identity. As a co-heir, you stand beside Jesus—not beneath Him in shame, but beside Him in grace. He shares His kingdom, His righteousness, and His Spirit with you. And just as He prayed in John 17, He gave you the very glory that the Father gave Him. That means the beauty, weight, and honor of His presence now rests on your life too.

This doesn't make you equal to Jesus in nature or divinity—but it does mean you are fully included in His inheritance. You don't wait for crumbs to fall from the table. You sit with the Son. You eat the bread of life, drink deeply of the Spirit, and walk in the power of the One who conquered death.

Being a co-heir also means sharing in His mission and His sufferings. We carry His heart. We love as He loves. We sometimes face rejection as He did. But all of it is wrapped in the assurance of shared glory—both now and forever.

You are not on the outside looking in. You are fully inside the inheritance of God because Jesus wanted you there. This is your position: seated with Him, robed in righteousness, and radiant with His glory.

Affirmation: Everything Jesus has, I share in. I am a joint heir—welcomed, included, and blessed with the riches of God's grace.

Prayer: Jesus, You didn't just forgive me or rescue me from judgment—you brought me into Your own inheritance. You gave me a seat with You. You welcomed me into everything You received from the Father. I don't deserve it. I didn't earn it. But You chose to include me anyway.

Thank You for sharing Your glory with me. Thank You for calling me family. You didn't hold anything back—not even Your own Spirit. Help me live like someone who truly belongs. Let this truth shape how I see myself—not as someone on the outside trying to get in, but as someone fully embraced, fully accepted, fully loved.

Teach me how to carry this honor with humility. Let Your inheritance change how I pray, how I respond to challenges, how I love people, and how I see my purpose. You've made me a joint heir—and I want to live like it, not for pride or comfort, but because I'm walking in what You paid for. Let this truth rise in me like leaven until it transforms everything I am. Amen.

28

HE MADE ME AN AMBASSADOR OF HIS KINGDOM

2 Corinthians 5:20 (NKJV) Now then, we are ambassadors for Christ, as though God were pleading through us: we implore you on Christ's behalf, be reconciled to God.

Matthew 5:14 (NIV) You are the light of the world. A town built on a hill cannot be hidden.

When you came into Christ, you didn't just receive salvation—you received a mission. Jesus didn't just wash you clean and leave you waiting for heaven. He filled you with His Spirit and sent you out as His representative. You are now an ambassador of His kingdom, carrying His message, His love, and His presence into the world around you.

An ambassador doesn't speak their own opinions—they speak on behalf of the One who sent them. That means when you speak words of reconciliation, love, and truth, it's as if God Himself is speaking through you. You've been entrusted with the message of the gospel—and empowered by the Spirit to deliver it with boldness, compassion, and grace.

But being an ambassador isn't about preaching on a street corner or having a microphone. It's about representing the heart of the King in your everyday life. Your kindness is kingdom. Your patience is kingdom. Your generosity, your peace, your forgiveness—these are the currency of heaven that you carry into the world.

Jesus said you are the light of the world—a city on a hill that cannot be hidden. That means your life is meant to be seen, not in self-promotion, but in radiant love that draws people to the Father. You don't have to manufacture that light—it's already in you. Just don't hide it. Don't shrink back. Let your life speak of Jesus.

This is not pressure—it's partnership. You don't represent God in your own strength. The Holy Spirit equips you, empowers you, and leads you. You're not an ambassador because you're perfect. You're an ambassador because He chose you, redeemed you, and filled you with His presence.

Your life has purpose. Your story has power. Your presence carries the fragrance of Christ to a world in need. You don't just belong to the kingdom—you represent it.

Affirmation: I represent heaven on earth. My words, my life, and my love reflect the heart of the King who sent me.

Prayer: Jesus, thank You for making me Your ambassador. You didn't just save me and leave me—you brought me into Your kingdom and gave me a mission. I'm humbled that You trust me to carry Your message. Thank You for empowering me with Your Spirit to walk in that purpose.

Help me remember that I speak for You—not in arrogance, but in love. Let my words carry Your kindness. Let my actions reflect Your mercy. Let my life shine with the hope and light of heaven. Whether I'm talking with family, working with coworkers, or crossing paths with strangers—let people see You in me.

29

HE PUT HIS SPIRIT IN AND UPON ME FOR POWER

Acts 1:8 (NKJV) But you shall receive power when the Holy Spirit has come upon you; and you shall be witnesses to Me in Jerusalem, and in all Judea and Samaria, and to the end of the earth.

Luke 4:18 (CSB) The Spirit of the Lord is on me, because he has anointed me to preach good news to the poor.

Jesus never intended for you to live the Christian life without power. He didn't save you and leave you to figure things out alone. When you believed, God revived your spirit and joined His Spirit to yours—not just to comfort you, but to empower you and live through you. God's Spirit is in you, to come upon you. That's what Jesus promised in Acts 1:8: the Spirit coming upon you to make you a bold, effective witness of the kingdom.

This anointing isn't for the spiritually elite—it's for every believer. It's for you. You've been given the same Spirit that raised Jesus from the dead (Romans 8:11), and He rests upon you for power, love, and action. When Jesus declared in Luke 4:18 that the Spirit of the Lord was upon Him, He was announcing His mission—and now, that same Spirit equips you to walk in His footsteps.

You don't have to muster up strength to love people. You don't have to force yourself to be brave, wise, or insightful. The Spirit empowers you. He gives you words when you need them, discernment when it counts, compassion when you feel dry, and boldness when you're afraid. He flows through your uniqueness—your personality, your voice, your life—with supernatural grace.

You are not powerless. You are not empty-handed. You are anointed to share good news, break oppression, pray with authority, serve with joy, walk in signs that point to Jesus, and release healing. The Spirit's power isn't for show—it's for fruit. It's for power. It's for love.

Let this truth shape your mindset. You are not just filled—you are equipped. You are not just saved—you are sent. You carry heaven's power into a hurting world, and the Spirit of the Lord is upon you.

Affirmation: I am not powerless. The Spirit of God is upon me to lead, comfort, empower, and fill me with boldness and wisdom.

Prayer: Holy Spirit, thank You for coming upon me with power. You're not just beside me—you live in me and rest upon me. You've anointed me, Jesus made me worthy to carry Your presence.

I receive Your power—not just to feel better, but to live on mission. Empower me to love boldly, speak clearly, serve humbly, and walk confidently. I need Your courage in hard conversations, Your insight when I'm unsure, and Your compassion when I feel empty. Thank You for always being ready to fill me again.

Remind me that I'm not powerless. Let me walk into every space knowing I carry Your presence. Let Your power flow through my life—not for my name, but for Jesus'. I don't want to hide or hesitate. I want to live like someone filled with fire and purpose. Thank You for trusting me with Your Spirit. I say yes again today. Amen.

30

HE SENDS ME TO THE WORLD TO GLORIFY GOD

John 17:18 (NIV) As you sent me into the world, I have sent them into the world.

Matthew 5:16 (NKJV) Let your light so shine before men, that they may see your good works and glorify your Father in heaven.

You weren't just saved *from* something—you were saved *for* something. Jesus didn't redeem you so you could sit back and wait for heaven. He made you new, filled and sealed you with His Spirit, and sent you back into the world with a mission: to reflect the Father's heart. Just as He was sent, so are you.

You are a light-bearer in a world that desperately needs the glow of truth, grace, and mercy. But your light doesn't come from your own strength—it comes from Christ in you. He's the source, and you're the vessel. Every act of kindness, every word of hope, every faithful choice you make becomes a lighthouse to illuminate the way to safe harbor in Christ.

Jesus glorified the Father by loving deeply, obeying completely, and serving humbly. Now He calls you to do the same—not through perfection, but through surrender. You glorify God when you forgive instead of holding grudges, when you choose peace over offense, when you stand in integrity when no one is watching. These moments matter. They shine.

And you don't have to do this alone. You've been empowered by the Holy Spirit to carry this mission with joy, confidence. and power. Whether you're in a crowded room or a quiet season, whether you're seen or unseen—your life still speaks. Your life still shines. Your presence in the world is intentional, and your good works point others to a good God.

This isn't about performance—it's about presence. God's presence in you. Jesus didn't just send you out; He goes with you. You don't need to chase a grand calling to bring Him glory—your everyday faithfulness is already a powerful testimony.

You've been sent to live, love, and shine in a way that glorifies your Father. Wherever you go today, remember—you are the evidence that God is real and good.

Affirmation: My life has a holy purpose—to glorify God in everything I do. I live for His glory, and His light shines through me.

Prayer: Jesus, thank You for sending me into the world with purpose. It humbles me to know that You trust me to reflect Your heart. I don't want to live for myself—I want to live for Your glory. Let my life speak of Your goodness, not just in big ways, but in the quiet daily moments that no one else sees.

Help me see the value in how I show up—in my family, my workplace, my conversations, my choices. Remind me that I don't have to try harder to shine; I just have to stay close to You. Let everything in me—my thoughts, my tone, my posture—reveal You. Use me today, Lord, not to impress, but to love. Be glorified in me. Amen.

31

HE GAVE ME ETERNAL LIFE

John 10:28 (NKJV) And I give them eternal life, and they shall never perish; neither shall anyone snatch them out of My hand.

John 17:3 (ESV) And this is eternal life, that they know you, the only true God, and Jesus Christ whom you have sent.

Eternal life isn't just about where you go when you die—it's about the life you've already received. It began the moment you believed. Jesus defined eternal life as knowing God, personally and intimately, through Him. It's not limited to your future in His celestial kingdom; it's yours now.

This life is not something you earn or maintain through effort—it's a gift Jesus freely gave. He said plainly, "I give them eternal life." Not temporary hope. Not a trial version of salvation. Eternal life. And He followed it with a promise: "They shall never perish; neither shall anyone snatch them out of My hand." That means your salvation is secure—not because you hold onto Him tightly, but because He holds onto you.

Eternal life isn't just endless—it's abundant. It's life filled with God's presence, peace, joy, and purpose. It's not marked by religious striving but by ongoing relationship. You are already living your forever with Him. And that forever is infused with His Spirit, His nearness, His goodness. Through His great and precious promises, made sure in the lifeblood of Christ, you can partake of Heaven on Earth.

Knowing God is not just part of your life—He *is* your life. Everything flows from that connection. Your identity, peace, direction, and strength are all rooted in the unbreakable union you now have with the Father through Jesus.

You don't have to fear being lost, abandoned, or cast out. Nothing can pluck you from His hand—not your mistakes, not your doubts, not your weakest days. Eternal life is as much about security as it is about duration. Jesus didn't give you a fragile salvation—He gave you Himself. And He's not letting go.

So today, rest in that assurance. Live from the confidence that you are safe in Him. Let eternal life shape how you see today—not just how you prepare for the future. Because the life of heaven is already inside you.

Affirmation: I already have eternal life—not just someday, but right now. I know God, and I walk in the fullness of life that never ends.

Prayer: Jesus, thank You for the gift of eternal life. Not just a promise for someday, but a reality I get to live in now. Thank You that knowing You is life—that Your presence is my forever, and my peace. I'm so grateful that nothing can take me out of Your hand. Not fear, not failure, not even death itself. You've secured me, and You've filled me with Your life.

Teach me to live each day aware of what I already have in You. Help me stop striving and start enjoying the relationship You paid everything to give me. Let Your life in me shape how I see the world, how I face hardship, and how I love others. I'm safe in You. I'm alive in You. And that will never change. Amen.

32

HE DIED SO I CAN LIVE

Romans 6:10 (NIV) The death he died, he died to sin once for all; but the life he lives, he lives to God.

2 Timothy 2:11 (NKJV) This is a faithful saying: For if we died with Him, we shall also live with Him.

Jesus didn't just rescue you from sin and death—He raised you into a new kind of life, one with an eternal purpose and direction. When you believed, something deeper than behavior changed—your very identity was transformed. You were spiritually united with Christ in His death, and now you share in His resurrected life. And that life has a focus: it is lived *to God*.

This means your new life is no longer about self-preservation, achievement, or striving for approval. It's about reflecting the love, holiness, and glory of the One who saved you. Just as Jesus now lives to the Father—completely yielded, completely victorious—you are invited into that same posture of surrender and power. You are no longer dead in sin, you are eternally alive in Christ because the Spirit of Christ is living in and through you, with the same quality of life Jesus enjoys.

You don't just live *from* Jesus' victory—you live *with* His mindset, His power, and His mission. This is the highest calling: to live each moment as a vessel of divine purpose, bringing heaven's presence into earthly places. Everything about your life—your time, talents, and relationships—can now be an expression of worship and partnership with God.

This kind of living isn't about religious performance. It's not about trying harder to be good. It's about living in deep, constant relationship with God—letting His Spirit shape your priorities, fill your moments, and fuel your actions. It means you're not waiting for eternity to start someday. You're already walking in it. Every decision, every step, every conversation can carry the fragrance of eternity when you live from this awareness.

You are no longer a slave to sin, fear, or your past. You are alive to God—responsive to His love, open to His leading, and secure in His presence. Jesus didn't raise you halfway. He brought you fully into His life so you could live with the same purpose: to glorify the Father, to love like heaven, and to walk as a citizen of eternity in a broken world.

Let that reality rise in you like leaven—quietly reshaping how you think, how you feel, and how you live each day. You are not just living—you are living *to God*.

Affirmation: Jesus gave His life so I could truly live. I don't live for myself anymore—I live by His life in me.

Prayer: Father, thank You that I have been raised to a life that matters. I don't belong to death anymore—I belong to You. My purpose is rooted in eternity, and my days are filled with Your presence. Help me live aware of this new life You've given me.

Let me respond to Your love with joy, obedience, and peace. Shape my decisions with Your wisdom. Let the life of Christ within me overflow into everything I touch. This life is Yours, Lord. I live to You—not out of duty, but out of delight. Thank You for calling me into Your eternal story. Amen.

33

HE TOOK AWAY MY SHAME

Hebrews 12:2 (NKJV) ...who for the joy that was set before Him endured the cross, despising the shame, and has sat down at the right hand of the throne of God.

Isaiah 61:7 (NIV) Instead of your shame you will receive a double portion, and instead of disgrace you will rejoice in your inheritance.

The Roman cross wasn't only an instrument of pain—it was a spectacle of humiliation. Jesus wasn't just crucified; He was stripped, mocked, spat on, and publicly dishonored. In every way, He bore the weight of shame—emotionally, spiritually, and physically. Why? So that you would never have to live under shame again.

Shame is different from guilt. Guilt says, "I did something wrong." Shame says, "There's something wrong with me." It isolates. It silences. It covers you in a false identity. But Jesus carried it all. He despised its power, endured its sting, and triumphed over it. What should have clung to you forever was nailed to Him instead.

This wasn't just forgiveness—it was redemption at the deepest level. Jesus didn't only remove your sins; He restored your honor. He didn't just wipe your slate clean—He clothed you in righteousness and raised your face to meet His without fear. You no longer need to hide. You no longer carry the labels of your past. You don't have to wear what others put on you.

Isaiah 61:7 isn't a distant promise—it's your new reality. Where you once carried shame, now you are crowned with honor. Where you were once afraid of being exposed, now you're invited into the light, fully known and fully loved.

This is the gospel: Jesus took your place in shame so you could take your place in glory. And now, His joy becomes your strength. His inheritance becomes your portion. His boldness becomes your freedom. Every trace of disgrace was absorbed by Him so that every part of you could be restored by Him.

You are not what you've done. You are not what was done to you. You are who Jesus says you are: restored, honored, and free.

Affirmation: Shame has no place in my story. Jesus bore it all and replaced it with honor, restoration, and identity.

Prayer: Jesus, You saw my shame and still chose the cross. You didn't turn away from the dishonor—I was the joy set before You. Thank You for enduring what I couldn't bear, for silencing every voice that told me I was unworthy. You didn't just remove my sin, You lifted my head.

I give You the shame I've carried—every label, every lie, every scar. I receive Your honor in its place. Let Your truth go deep. Remind me every day that I am covered in Your righteousness, not condemnation. I am not hidden anymore—I am healed. Thank You for restoring my dignity and rewriting my story. I walk in the light now, because You walked through the dark for me. Amen.

34

HE REMOVED THE RECORD OF MY WRONGS

Colossians 2:14 (NIV) Having canceled the charge of our legal indebtedness, which stood against us and condemned us; he has taken it away, nailing it to the cross.

Psalm 103:12 (NKJV) As far as the east is from the west, so far has He removed our transgressions from us.

Every sin had a ledger. Every failure had a file. But Jesus didn't come to manage your guilt—He came to delete it. On the cross, He didn't just absorb your punishment. He removed the record itself. The entire list of charges that rightfully condemned you was nailed to that wood and buried in His death.

There's no trace left. No paperwork waiting in heaven. No shadow of your past tucked in a drawer. When God looks at your record, He sees only Christ. Not even the accuser has access to what was erased.

The blood of Jesus didn't just cover your sins—it canceled the entire case against you.

This changes everything. You don't have to live under the weight of your past anymore. You don't have to overcompensate with good works or prove your worth. The cross already settled the verdict. You're not walking toward freedom—you're walking from it.

Psalm 103 says your transgressions have been removed "as far as the east is from the west." That's not a clever metaphor—it's a spiritual reality. In God's eyes, they are eternally distant, unrecoverable, unreachable. This is what grace does. It not only forgives—it forgets.

You don't have to live like you're on spiritual probation. You're not defined by your worst days. You're not carrying a spiritual rap sheet. You're clean. Your identity is no longer sinner trying to do better—it's saint made new in Christ.

And when guilt tries to creep back in—when the voice of accusation whispers old failures—you can answer with truth: "That record was nailed to the cross. That's not who I am anymore." Jesus didn't partially clear your name—He gave you His.

Affirmation: Every accusation against me has been erased. My past no longer defines me—grace does.

Prayer: Jesus, I'm in awe of what You did for me. You didn't just forgive me—you erased the entire record of my sin. You didn't file it away or hold it over my head. You nailed it to the cross and declared me free.

Help me live like someone whose slate is truly clean. Silence every accusing thought with Your truth. Remind me that I stand in Your righteousness, not my regret. Thank You for not just removing my guilt, but restoring my confidence. I believe You when You say it's finished—and I choose to walk in that freedom today. Amen.

35

HE MADE ME RIGHTEOUS

Romans 5:1 (NKJV) Therefore, having been justified by faith, we have peace with God through our Lord Jesus Christ.

Philippians 3:9 (NLT) I no longer count on my own righteousness through obeying the law; rather, I become righteous through faith in Christ. For God's way of making us right with Himself depends on faith.

To be righteous means you are as you should be with God. You are not righteous because of what you do —you are righteous because of who you trust. Righteousness is not a reward for performance. It is a gift that comes through faith in Jesus. The moment you believed, you were justified—declared right with God, not by your works, but by His grace.

To be justified means more than forgiven—it means declared innocent, as if the sin never existed. This isn't a temporary pardon—it's a permanent position. God doesn't relate to you based on your past. He sees you through the obedience of Christ. Jesus' perfect righteousness has been credited to your account. You don't have to earn it. You simply receive it.

Because of this, you now live in peace with God, not tension. There's no pressure to perform for approval or clean yourself up to be accepted. You're already approved, already accepted, already clean—because of faith. God isn't holding anything against you. You're not under condemnation—you're under grace.

This truth transforms how you live. It doesn't make you careless—it makes you confident. Righteousness by faith leads to rest, but it also leads to passion. You don't strive to be loved—you live from love. You don't obey to become righteous—you obey because you already are. Your relationship with God is not built on what you can do for Him, but on what He already did for you.

When you truly believe you're righteous by faith, you stop measuring yourself by your highs and lows. You stop asking, "Have I done enough?" and start living in the freedom of "Jesus did it all." That's not pride—that's gospel humility. It's the joyful confidence of someone who knows their place in the Father's heart.

Affirmation: I am not trying to become righteous—I am righteous by faith. It is finished, and I rest in that truth.

Prayer: Jesus, thank You for making me righteous by faith. You didn't ask me to prove myself—You asked me to trust You. I don't have to rely on my effort or good behavior to be accepted. You've already given me Your righteousness, and I receive it with a grateful heart.

Help me live every day aware of my right standing with the Father. Let that truth silence my doubts, quiet my fears, and fuel my love for You. I don't have to earn what You freely gave—I get to enjoy it. Teach me to rest in grace and walk boldly in Your peace. Amen.

36

HE RECONCILED ME TO GOD

2 Corinthians 5:18 (NLT) And all of this is a gift from God, who brought us back to Himself through Christ. And God has given us this task of reconciling people to him.

Colossians 1:21–22 (NKJV) And you, who once were alienated and enemies in your mind by wicked works, yet now He has reconciled in the body of His flesh through death, to present you holy, and blameless, and above reproach in His sight.

Sin didn't just separate us from God and strand our spirits in the realm of death—it made us feel like His enemies in our own minds. It twisted how we saw Him and how we saw ourselves. Fear, shame, and a sense of unworthiness kept us from drawing near, even though God's heart was always turned toward us. We felt distant—not because He pushed us away, but because we were dead in our sin and our sin distorted our perception of His love.

But Jesus didn't wait for us to come crawling back. He didn't demand we clean ourselves up or prove our sincerity. He came after us. He crossed the divide, took our guilt upon Himself, and tore down the wall that stood between us and God. Through His death, He didn't just open a door—He carried us through it. He brought us back home.

Reconciliation means there's nothing left standing between you and God. The war is over. The offense is gone. God isn't counting your sins against you—He's counting you as His own. And more than that, He doesn't just tolerate you—He treasures you. He died for you in spite of you being trapped in sin. He presents you before Himself as holy, blameless, and above reproach. That's not poetic exaggeration—it's your standing in Christ.

You are fully embraced. You are welcomed without hesitation. You don't have to earn your way into God's presence or apologize your way into His affection. He already settled everything that needed settling. Now He invites you to live as someone who is truly, fully accepted.

And this truth goes even further—because you've been reconciled, you're now entrusted with the message of reconciliation. You get to live your life as proof that peace with God is possible. Your freedom becomes someone else's invitation.

Even when your feelings falter or old accusations try to creep in, remember: your reconciliation is not up for debate. It's done. Finished. Irrevocable. God is not mad at you. He's not waiting to be impressed. He's already drawn you close—and He delights in keeping you there.

You're not trying to fix a broken relationship—Jesus already restored it. Live like someone who's at peace with God, because in Him, you truly are.

Affirmation: I'm not estranged or distant—I'm fully reconciled. God and I are in perfect relationship because of Jesus.

Prayer: Father, thank You for reconciling me through Jesus. Thank You that I'm no longer separated but brought near. I trust that You hold nothing against me. I let go of fear, guilt, and any sense of rejection—and I receive Your embrace. Even when I feel distant, remind me that You already closed the gap. Help me live every day from this place of peace. Let Your love shape how I see myself and how I treat others. You've made peace with me, and now I choose to walk in that peace with joy, freedom, and confidence. Amen.

37

HE MADE ME HOLY AND BLAMELESS

Ephesians 1:4 (NKJV) Just as He chose us in Him before the foundation of the world, that we should be holy and without blame before Him in love.

Colossians 1:22 (NLT) Yet now he has reconciled you to himself through the death of Christ in his physical body. As a result, he has brought you into his own presence, and you are holy and blameless as you stand before him without a single fault.

God didn't just save you from something—He saved you for something. From the very beginning, before the world was even formed, He chose you in love to be holy and without blame in His sight. This wasn't an afterthought. His plan was always to cleanse you so completely through Jesus that nothing could stand between you and His love. And now, because of what Christ has done, that plan is fulfilled. You are holy. You are blameless. You are without a single fault in God's eyes.

This holiness isn't something you grow into with good behavior. It's not a prize for perfect performance. It's your present identity, gifted to you by grace. Holiness means you are set apart, made clean, and fully accepted. Blameless means that no charge can be brought against you—not by the enemy, not by others, and not by your own guilty conscience. You've been washed, justified, and declared innocent.

God is not looking at your life through the lens of failure or struggle. He sees you through the finished work of His Son. When He looks at you, He sees someone worthy of love, fully accepted, radiant with righteousness. You are not what you used to be. You are not the sum of your mistakes. In Christ, you are completely new—and completely clean.

This truth doesn't lead to apathy; it leads to awe. When you truly believe that you are holy and blameless, you stop trying to earn your place and start living from it. You approach God with boldness, not hesitation. You silence shame with truth. You stop identifying with your past and begin identifying with Christ. You speak to yourself with grace. You treat others with mercy. You live differently—not to become holy, but because you already are.

In Christ, you are already holy. You are already blameless. God is not waiting for you to prove yourself—He's inviting you to live from the identity He's already given.

Affirmation: In Christ, I am holy and blameless. God looks at me through the lens of His Son and sees no fault in me.

Prayer: Father, thank You that I stand before You holy and blameless—not because of what I've done, but because of what Jesus has done for me. Thank You that when You look at me, You see someone without a single fault. I receive this identity by faith. Teach me to renew my mind daily and live in alignment with the purity You've already placed within me. Let this truth shape how I see myself, how I speak, how I respond to failure, and how I walk with You. I silence every lie that tells me I'm still dirty or distant. I am clean. I am close. I am chosen. I am Yours. Amen.

38

HE GAVE ME HIS OWN RIGHTEOUSNESS

2 Corinthians 5:21 (NKJV) For He made Him who knew no sin to be sin for us, that we might become the righteousness of God in Him.

Romans 3:22 (NLT) We are made right with God by placing our faith in Jesus Christ. And this is true for everyone who believes, no matter who we are.

Jesus didn't just remove your sin—He replaced it with something glorious. He gave you His own righteousness. Righteous means "as you should be." God made you as you should be through Christ. This wasn't a symbolic gesture or a temporary covering. It was a full and eternal exchange. He became sin so you could become righteousness. The spotless One took on your guilt, and in return, gave you His innocence. Not earned. Not achieved. Just received.

You don't have to beg for righteousness or try to maintain it through perfect performance. You have it —fully, now, and forever. When God looks at you, He sees the righteousness of His Son. He's not measuring your worth by your worst moment. He's honoring the finished work of Jesus in you. You are His handiwork, the product of His righteousness. You are not cycling between clean and dirty, accepted and rejected. You are secure in a righteousness that cannot be undone.

This righteousness is not based on behavior—it's based on nature. The very moment you believed, you were made new. Your spirit was translated from darkness to light and you became compatible with God's holiness. And from that right standing comes a new way of living—not driven by guilt or shame, but by confidence and joy. You don't strive to be righteous; you live because you are righteous. Even on your hardest days, righteousness is still your core identity. Nothing you face can undo what Christ has made you to be.

This changes everything—from how you pray to how you face failure. Instead of hiding in shame, you can come boldly before God, knowing you're already accepted. Instead of chasing perfection, you can rest in grace and grow from a place of security. You're not just covered—you're re-created.

So speak that truth. Think from that truth. Let it renew your mind, silence self-condemnation, and fill you with peace. Say it out loud if you need to: *I am the righteousness of God in Christ. I've been given*

His righteousness, and I live from that truth every day.

Affirmation: I wear the righteousness of Jesus Himself. I don't need to perform—I simply believe and receive.

Prayer: Jesus, thank You for giving me Your righteousness. You didn't just clean me up—you made me brand new. I'm not trying to earn what You've already given. I receive it with a grateful heart. Let this truth settle deep in me and shape how I see myself every single day. Remind me that I don't live from guilt—I live from grace. When I feel weak, remind me of who I truly am in You. Help me walk in this identity with boldness and humility. Because I am righteous in You, I can live free. Amen.

39

HE QUALIFIED ME TO SHARE IN HIS INHERITANCE

Colossians 1:12 (NKJV) Giving thanks to the Father who has qualified us to be partakers of the inheritance of the saints in the light.

Ephesians 1:11 (NLT) Furthermore, because we are united with Christ, we have received an inheritance from God.

Romans 8:17 (NKJV) And if children, then heirs—heirs of God and joint heirs with Christ, if indeed we suffer with Him, that we may also be glorified together.

You don't have to qualify yourself—God already did that through Jesus. The pressure to earn your place is over. Through Christ, you've been adopted, accepted, and brought into the full rights of sonship. You're not just forgiven—you're included. You're not just saved from judgment—you've been welcomed into the family blessing.

In God's kingdom, inheritance isn't based on performance—it's based on identity. And your identity is now found in Christ. You've been united with Him, made righteous by His blood, and sealed with His Spirit. That means your name is written into God's will, and nothing can revoke it. Jesus has become the heir of all things, and you are a joint kingdom heir, with and in Him. It pleases God to give you His kingdom - to give you Christ's quality of life.

Being qualified means you're no longer disqualified —not by sin, not by your past, not by your struggles. God doesn't hand out spiritual blessings based on merit; He gives them based on union. And if you're in Christ, then everything He has is yours too. His peace is yours. His authority is yours. His joy, His victory, His access to the Father—all of it is part of your inheritance. You don't inherit in part—you inherit in full.

And here's the beautiful part: you're not just an heir of God—you're a joint heir with Jesus. That means God didn't hold anything back from you. The same love, favor, and access that belong to Jesus now belong to you. You've been invited into the same glory, the same relationship, and the same inheritance. It just keeps getting better.

You don't have to beg or wonder if you're worthy—you only need to believe that Jesus is worthy, and you are in Him. The more convinced you become of this truth, the more boldly you'll receive what's already yours. You are not a spiritual outsider—you are an heir, fully qualified, fully included, and deeply loved.

Affirmation: I am not disqualified by my past. God has qualified me through Christ, and I fully share in the inheritance of the saints.

Prayer: Father, thank You for qualifying me—not because of anything I've done, but because of what Jesus finished. You didn't just save me, You welcomed me into Your family and made me a full heir. I don't have to earn my place—I already belong. Thank You that I'm not just an heir of blessing, but a joint heir with Jesus. I share in His victory, His favor, and His access to You. Help me truly believe that nothing disqualifies me in Your eyes. Let me live like someone who carries the inheritance of heaven: with confidence, generosity, and joy. I receive it all with gratitude—Your peace, Your presence, Your promises. Teach me to walk in the fullness of what You've freely given. Amen.

40

HE DELIVERED ME FROM DARKNESS

Colossians 1:13 (NKJV) He has delivered us from the power of darkness and conveyed us into the kingdom of the Son of His love.

John 8:12 (NIV) When Jesus spoke again to the people, he said, "I am the light of the world. Whoever follows me will never walk in darkness, but will have the light of life."

Before Christ, we lived under the dominion of darkness—ruled by fear, shame, deception, addiction, guilt, confusion, and spiritual death. We were bound by sin's grip and blinded to the truth. But Jesus didn't just enter the darkness—He shattered its power. He didn't come to negotiate with darkness. He came to destroy it and deliver you.

The word "delivered" in Colossians 1:13 is past tense. It's already happened. Jesus didn't leave you halfway between darkness and light. He transferred you fully into His kingdom—a kingdom ruled not by fear or guilt, but by love and truth. You were rescued from one dominion and fully placed into another.

This wasn't a subtle shift—it was a radical relocation. You've been relocated spiritually, permanently, and completely.

You no longer live under the shadow of condemnation. You don't answer to your past anymore. You don't owe anything to fear, addiction, or shame. The domain of darkness has no legal claim on you. You are not just visiting the light—you belong there now. And in that light, everything changes. You can see clearly. You can walk freely. You can live boldly.

The "light of life" that Jesus gives is not just illumination—it's restoration. It brings direction, peace, and healing to areas that once felt hopeless. You don't have to wander anymore. You don't have to live with spiritual amnesia, forgetting who you are. You've been rescued, renamed, and relocated.

So when old habits try to creep in, when fear whispers or shame calls your name, remember—you've been delivered. Your location has changed. You're not striving to escape darkness; you're learning to walk confidently in the light you already possess. You are no longer a slave. You are a citizen of the kingdom of the Son of His love.

Affirmation: I have been rescued from the power of darkness and transferred into the kingdom of light. I walk in truth, love, and freedom.

Prayer: Jesus, thank You for rescuing me from the grip of darkness. You didn't just shine a light into my confusion—you pulled me out completely and placed me in Your kingdom of love. I don't belong to fear, shame, or guilt anymore. I belong to You. Help me see every situation in light of my new identity. Teach me how to walk in freedom, not striving for it but living from it. Let Your truth, peace, and joy flood every part of my life. I welcome Your light to lead me, heal me, and shine through me. I am free because of You—and I choose to live like it. Amen.

41

HE GAVE ME THE LIGHT OF LIFE

John 8:12 (NKJV) Then Jesus spoke to them again, saying, "I am the light of the world. He who follows Me shall not walk in darkness, but have the light of life."

Psalm 27:1 (NIV) The Lord is my light and my salvation—whom shall I fear?

Jesus didn't just shine *at* you—He moved in. He is the Light of the world, and when you follow Him, His light becomes your own. He doesn't hand you a flashlight and wish you luck—He walks with you, illuminating every step with His presence. You don't walk *toward* the light anymore—you walk *in* it. And this light is not weak, flickering, or temporary. It's eternal, radiant, and deeply personal. You now carry the light of life within you because Christ Himself lives in you.

This light doesn't just expose the darkness—it heals what's been hidden there. It reveals the lies you once believed and replaces them with truth. It reveals the love of the Father, the grace of Jesus, and the nearness of the Spirit. It shines into the places you thought were too dark for healing, too confusing for peace, or too painful for restoration. And in the light of Jesus, you see yourself clearly—not as broken and unworthy, but as redeemed, valuable, and empowered. Fear loses its grip in the presence of that kind of light. Shame melts away. The path ahead becomes clearer—not because you control it all, but because you trust the One who never leaves your side.

His light doesn't just help you avoid darkness—it fills you with joy, purpose, and confidence. You're not fumbling your way through life—you're being led by the Light of Life Himself. You are no longer a prisoner to your past, your mistakes, or your fear of the unknown. He is your clarity in confusion, your peace in anxiety, and your joy in the midst of sorrow.

Psalm 27 reminds you that the Lord is both your light *and* your salvation. He strengthens you when you're tired. He keeps you safe when fear tries to creep in. That's why you don't have to live afraid. The same God who lights your path also guards your heart.

You don't walk in dimness anymore. You walk in full access to the light of life. And everywhere you go, that light shines through you. Your presence carries hope. Your words carry truth. Your life reflects the One who called you out of darkness and into His marvelous light. The more you walk in it, the more others will see it too—and they'll be drawn not just to you, but to Him.

Affirmation: Jesus is my light, and now His light lives in me. I don't walk in confusion or fear—I walk in clarity, purpose, and radiant hope.

Prayer: Jesus, thank You for being the Light of the world—and the Light in my life. Because of You, I don't have to live confused, ashamed, or afraid. You lead me, You're with me, and You shine through me. I don't want to hide, shrink back, or wander—I want to walk fully in the light You've given. Help me walk in Your light every day—with clarity in my decisions, peace in my emotions, and joy in my steps. Let Your light not only guide me but also overflow from me, touching others with the hope and truth I've found in You. I'm grateful, Lord—so grateful. Amen.

42

HE BROKE THE POWER OF FEAR

2 Timothy 1:7 (NKJV) For God has not given us a spirit of fear, but of power and of love and of a sound mind.

Hebrews 2:15 (NLT) Only in this way could he set free all who have lived their lives as slaves to the fear of dying.

Fear was once your master—but Jesus broke its power. Through His death and resurrection, He didn't just forgive your sin—He shattered the grip of fear. That includes the biggest fear of all: the fear of death. He didn't avoid it—He faced it head-on and came out victorious, so you could live free. You're not under fear's authority anymore. The chains that used to hold you don't get the final say.

Fear isn't just an emotion—it's a spiritual influence that tries to paralyze, deceive, and limit. But you've been given something far greater. God placed His own Spirit within you, and that Spirit isn't timid or fragile. It's the Spirit of power—the strength of God Himself. It's the Spirit of love—the perfect love that casts out fear. And it's the Spirit of a sound mind—clear, stable, anchored in truth. You're not losing your mind—you've been given the mind of Christ.

This means you don't have to live reactionary or on edge, bracing for what might go wrong. Even when fear whispers worst-case scenarios, you can answer with faith-filled truth. Jesus has already overcome the thing you're afraid of. Whether it's fear of failure, fear of rejection, fear of the unknown, or fear of not being enough—He's already gone ahead of you and declared victory.

You are no longer a slave to fear. You are a child of God, empowered to live bold and free. That freedom doesn't come from pretending fear isn't real—it comes from knowing fear isn't in charge anymore. You've been given power to stand firm, love to reach out, and a sound mind to stay clear when the world feels chaotic.

Jesus didn't just die to set you free from sin—He set you free from fear. And when you walk in that freedom, you carry the confidence of heaven with you into every situation.

Affirmation: I do not have a spirit of fear—I have power, love, and a sound mind. Jesus broke fear's grip on me, and I walk in boldness and freedom.

Prayer: Jesus, thank You for breaking the power of fear in my life. You faced death so I wouldn't have to fear it. You were rejected so I could be fully accepted. You gave me a new Spirit—full of power, full of love, and full of clarity. I don't want to live like a slave to fear anymore. Let Your boldness rise in me today. Help me choose courage over worry, love over self-protection, truth over lies. When fear tries to creep in, remind me of what You've already done. I'm not stuck. I'm not fragile. I'm free—and I'm walking forward with You. Amen.

43

HE TOOK MY PUNISHMENT SO I COULD HAVE PEACE WITH GOD

Isaiah 53:5 (NIV) But he was pierced for our transgressions, he was crushed for our iniquities; the punishment that brought us peace was on him, and by his wounds we are healed.

Romans 5:1 (NKJV) Therefore, having been justified by faith, we have peace with God through our Lord Jesus Christ.

John 14:27 (NKJV) Peace I leave with you, My peace I give to you; not as the world gives do I give to you. Let not your heart be troubled, neither let it be afraid.

Jesus didn't just suffer physically—He took the full punishment that sin demanded. Not because He deserved it, but because we did. And the result? Peace. Real peace. Soul-deep, God-given peace.

This peace is not temporary or fragile. It is a settled reality between you and God. The punishment that brought you peace was already poured out—there's nothing left for you to bear. You are no longer walking under wrath or waiting for reconciliation. Through Jesus, peace has been fully purchased, and it is your new foundation.

That peace is more than a feeling—it's a position. The peace Jesus gives is more than a tranquil state of mind, it's a restored relationship with God almighty, maker of all things. You now stand in a place of divine favor, not condemnation. You're not trying to make things right with God—Jesus already did. Your relationship with Him is whole. You are fully accepted, fully known, and fully loved.

And that peace doesn't just stay between you and God. It flows into your inner world. It calms anxiety. It quiets the chaos. It gives you permission to stop striving and simply *be*—anchored in grace, rooted in love. Even in life's hardest moments, this peace remains. It becomes your guide, your guard, and your grounding.

You don't need to wonder where you stand. You've been justified by faith. And because of that, you have peace with God through Jesus Christ. And the peace that he gives remains.

Affirmation:
I have peace with God. Jesus took my punishment so I could live whole, free, and fully accepted. His

work is enough. I am no longer condemned—I am at peace with God.

Prayer:
Jesus, thank You for taking what I deserved and giving me what I never could earn—peace. Thank You that because of You, I am not at odds with God but completely reconciled. I don't have to live under fear, shame, or judgment anymore. I rest in Your finished work. Let Your peace settle into every part of my heart and overflow through me today—in my thoughts, in my words, and in how I treat others. Teach me to live anchored in Your peace. Amen.

44

HE GAVE ME HIS VICTORY OVER THE WORLD

John 16:33 (NKJV) These things I have spoken to you, that in Me you may have peace. In the world you will have tribulation; but be of good cheer, I have overcome the world.

1 John 5:4 (CSB) Because everyone who has been born of God conquers the world. This is the victory that has conquered the world: our faith.

Jesus faced the full weight of the world's brokenness —temptation, pressure, injustice, rejection—and overcame it. He didn't escape the world. He triumphed within it. And now, that victory is yours.

You're not just a believer—you're an overcomer. Jesus didn't leave you behind to figure things out on your own. He clothed you in His triumph. The same power that raised Him from the dead now lives in you. And that means you don't just survive—you overcome.

This doesn't mean life will be easy. Jesus was clear: tribulation is part of the journey. But He was also clear about something else—you have peace in Him and victory through Him. That means when life feels chaotic, your peace isn't shaken. And when it feels like you're surrounded by setbacks, you still have a way forward.

Faith isn't pretending the struggle isn't real. It's knowing the outcome is already settled. You're not trying to win—you're living from the win Jesus already secured. Your role isn't to strive harder but to believe deeper—to let His finished work define your perspective and fuel your perseverance.

You're not powerless in your battles. You've been given overcoming faith, and that faith connects you to a victory that cannot be undone. You don't fight for acceptance—you fight from identity. You don't push for victory—you walk in what's already yours. And every time you trust Him, you enforce His triumph in your life.

Even in the moments that feel messy or unresolved, you are still covered in His victory. The world may press in, but it cannot overpower the One who lives in you. His overcoming Spirit makes you resilient, hopeful, and victorious in all things.

Affirmation:

Jesus has overcome the world, and I share in His victory. I don't strive to win—I live from the win. No matter what I face, I am more than a conqueror through Him.

Prayer:

Jesus, thank You for overcoming everything I'll ever face. Your victory is my anchor. Even when things feel overwhelming, I trust that You've already gone ahead of me and won. Help me to stay grounded in that truth. Let me respond to life's challenges with faith, not fear—with joy, not stress. I choose to live from Your triumph, confident that I am more than a conqueror in You. Amen.

45

HE GAVE ME THE POWER TO OVERCOME SIN

Romans 6:14 (NKJV) For sin shall not have dominion over you, for you are not under law but under grace.

Titus 2:11–12 (NIV) For the grace of God has appeared that offers salvation to all people. It teaches us to say "No" to ungodliness and worldly passions, and to live self-controlled, upright and godly lives in this present age.

Jesus didn't just take the penalty for your sin—He took away its power. He didn't leave you forgiven but stuck. He made you free and powerful through His Spirit.

Grace is more than mercy—it's divine strength. It's not just a covering for failure; it's the inner working of God that lifts you into freedom. Because of Jesus, sin is no longer your master. You don't live under law—trying and failing and trying again. You live under grace, where God Himself empowers you from the inside out.

Sin may tempt you, but it no longer owns you. You are free to choose righteousness, not by willpower, but by the Spirit's power within you. Grace doesn't just excuse your past—it empowers your present and secures your future. The more you renew your mind to this truth, the more naturally freedom becomes your way of life.

You don't have to stay stuck in patterns that once defined you. You're not powerless to temptation. When old habits or thoughts come knocking, grace gives you the boldness to shut the door. The Holy Spirit within you leads, convicts, and strengthens—not to condemn, but to remind you that you're free.

And even when you stumble, grace doesn't shame you—it lifts you. It reminds you that your sin doesn't disqualify you; it reminds you of your identity and calls you higher. You are not walking this road alone. You're walking in step with the Spirit who empowers you day by day.

Sin may try to whisper lies about who you are, but you're under a louder truth: you are the righteousness of God in Christ. You're not a slave to cycles, shame, or self-effort. You've been equipped with resurrection power. The same Spirit who raised

Jesus from the dead lives in you—and He is more than enough.

Affirmation:
Sin has no dominion over me. I'm not under law—I'm under grace. I walk in freedom and power because the Spirit of God lives in me.

Prayer:
Father, thank You for giving me real, lasting freedom. I'm not trapped, I'm not weak, and I'm not defined by my past. You've filled me with Your Spirit and broken sin's control over me. Let Your grace teach me, guide me, and strengthen me every day. When I feel tempted or overwhelmed, remind me who I really am—free, righteous, and loved. I choose to live from the truth of who I am in Christ—free, empowered, and whole. Amen.

46

HE GAVE ME A NEW IDENTITY

2 Corinthians 5:17 (NKJV) Therefore, if anyone is in Christ, he is a new creation; old things have passed away; behold, all things have become new.

Galatians 2:20 (CSB) I have been crucified with Christ, and I no longer live, but Christ lives in me. The life I now live in the body, I live by faith in the Son of God, who loved me and gave himself for me.

When you believed in Jesus, you didn't just get a clean slate—you received a brand-new identity. Your old self, shaped by sin, shame, fear, and failure, was nailed to the cross with Christ. You're not trying to fix the old you—you are a whole new being. A brand-new you was created, born of God, full of His Spirit, and rooted in His righteousness.

This new identity isn't something you work toward—it's something you live from. You are righteous, accepted, deeply loved, and completely made new in Him. God isn't waiting for you to become worthy—He already made you worthy by placing you in Christ. Your worth is no longer based on performance or perfection; it's based on the One who gave His life for you.

The enemy may try to tempt you with your old mindset or remind you of your past, but those things no longer define you. You've been relocated—from sin to righteousness, from striving to resting, from shame to sonship.

Christ lives in you now. That means His peace is in you. His authority is in you. His power, love, and holiness are alive in your spirit. You don't have to live trying to earn or prove who you are—you get to rest in who He says you already are. Every label the world or your past tried to stick to you falls off in light of your new creation identity.

Let go of old labels and lies. You are not who you used to be, and you never will be again. You are not the sum of your mistakes, your struggles, or your history. You are a child of God—called, clean, and capable of reflecting His glory in everyday life. This identity is secure, unshakable, and eternal—and the more you believe it, the more naturally you'll live like it.

Affirmation:
I am a new creation in Christ. My old self is gone. I live by faith in the One who gave Himself for me. I

don't live trying to become—I live as one who already is.

Prayer:
Jesus, thank You for making me brand new. You didn't just forgive me—you changed who I am at the core. I'm not stuck in the old anymore. I receive my identity in You, and I choose to see myself the way You do: whole, righteous, loved, and free. When lies come to accuse me, remind me that I've already been raised with You. Let me live from this truth, speak from this truth, and love from this truth. Teach me to trust what You say about me more than what I feel or fear. Thank You for making me new. I'm so grateful. Amen.

47

HE GAVE ME BOLD ACCESS TO THE FATHER

Hebrews 4:16 (NKJV) Let us therefore come boldly to the throne of grace, that we may obtain mercy and find grace to help in time of need.

Ephesians 3:12 (NIV) In him and through faith in him we may approach God with freedom and confidence.

Romans 5:2 (NLT) Because of our faith, Christ has brought us into this place of undeserved privilege where we now stand, and we confidently and joyfully look forward to sharing God's glory.

Because of Jesus, you don't approach God with fear —you come boldly. You are no longer a distant outsider or hesitant servant. You are a beloved child with full access to the Father's heart, presence, and help. He doesn't merely tolerate you—He welcomes you with joy. You're not sneaking in the back door of heaven—you're walking through the front gate with your head held high, hand in hand with Jesus.

This isn't a throne of judgment for you—it's a throne of grace. You don't have to wait until you've had a good week, fixed your attitude, or gotten your life in order. You're not graded when you pray. You're invited. And every time you come near, you find what you need most: mercy for your mess and grace for your journey.

Faith in Christ gives you that access. It's not based on your performance, your eloquence, or your record—it's based entirely on Jesus. Your connection is secure because He secured it. Even in your weakness, confusion, or weariness, you belong in the presence of God. He is never too busy, too distant, or too disappointed to meet with you. He calls you near—and He means it.

God wants you close. Your questions, your fears, your joys, your needs—they all belong in His presence. Jesus didn't die so you could stand at a distance. He died so you could come near with confidence, knowing that mercy is available and grace is already flowing toward you. Bold access isn't prideful—it's a humble confidence in what Jesus already accomplished.

Affirmation:
I have bold access to the Father. I come confidently, knowing I'm welcome, loved, and heard.

Prayer:

Father, thank You for the invitation to come boldly. Thank You that I don't have to tiptoe into Your presence—I can run to You. Thank You for grace that always meets me and mercy that never runs out. Let me live from this place of closeness and joy. Remind me daily that I'm already accepted, already welcomed, and already heard. When I'm unsure of what to say, remind me that You just want me near. And when I need help, let me run to You first—because I know You'll be there. Amen.

48

HE GAVE ME THE MIND OF CHRIST

1 Corinthians 2:16 (NKJV) For "who has known the mind of the Lord that he may instruct Him?" But we have the mind of Christ.

Romans 12:2 (NLT) Don't copy the behavior and customs of this world, but let God transform you into a new person by changing the way you think. Then you will learn to know God's will for you, which is good and pleasing and perfect.

Jesus didn't just save your soul—He gave you a new heart and you can now renew your mind. The same Spirit that raised Him from the dead now empowers you to think with His wisdom, His clarity, and His peace. You have the mind of Christ. That's not a metaphor or a lofty idea—it's a spiritual reality. You now have access to heaven's perspective in your everyday life.

You don't have to be stuck in fear-based thinking, old assumptions, or anxious loops. God is actively renewing your thoughts, not by force but by grace. The more you engage His Word and yield to the

Spirit, the more your thoughts come into alignment with truth. And with that alignment comes peace, stability, and purpose. The mind of Christ is not reactive or confused. It is calm, sure, discerning, and centered in love.

Having the mind of Christ doesn't mean you'll never have a negative thought—but it means you're no longer a slave to them. You can now filter your thoughts through God's truth instead of your past or your pain. You are empowered to pause, to reflect, and to respond with wisdom. The mind of Christ leads you away from striving and into rest. It silences shame, anchors identity, and gives you eyes to see what God sees.

You've been given something priceless—His very mindset. Not just for church moments, but for daily decisions, for relational challenges, for everything. His thoughts shape your words, influence your choices, and transform your inner world.

Affirmation:
I have the mind of Christ. My thoughts are being renewed daily. I think with clarity, truth, peace, and purpose.

Prayer:
Jesus, thank You for giving me Your mind. I don't have to be tossed around by fear or confusion

anymore. You've given me Your perspective, Your peace, and Your wisdom. Help me recognize when I'm slipping back into old ways of thinking, and remind me that I've been made new. I choose today to think from truth—not from fear. I yield my thoughts to You. Teach me to see life through Your eyes, to speak from Your heart, and to walk in the calm, steady power of Your truth. Amen.

49

HE SEATED ME IN HEAVENLY PLACES

Ephesians 2:6 (NKJV) and raised us up together, and made us sit together in the heavenly places in Christ Jesus.

Colossians 3:1 (NLT) Since you have been raised to new life with Christ, set your sights on the realities of heaven, where Christ sits in the place of honor at God's right hand.

Jesus isn't the only one to raise from the realm of death—He brought you with Him. When He ascended, He made it possible for you to ascended spiritually with Him. Now you're seated with Him in heavenly places. This isn't just a poetic idea or distant promise—it's your present spiritual reality. You are no longer defined by earthly limitations or ruled by the chaos of this world. Your citizenship is in heaven, and your life is hidden with Christ in God.

To be seated with Christ means you've been given a position of rest, authority, and unshakable identity. You're not running toward victory—you're living from it. You're not trying to get into Heaven—you're living from it. You're not trying to find your place—you've been given one. At the right hand of God is the place of honor and authority, and that's where you are in Christ. It means you have access to God, peace with God, and power through God—all because of Jesus.

You are seated, not striving. You are reigning, not surviving. Earth may try to tell you you're under it all, but heaven reminds you—you're above it in Him. From this place, your prayers shift from desperation to declaration. Your battles shift from being overwhelmed to being overcomers. You're not fighting for a breakthrough—you're enforcing what Jesus already won.

Living from heavenly places changes your posture. It gives you clarity in confusion, calm in the storm, and courage when the world feels shaky. It repositions your heart to trust and your mind to stay fixed on truth. And it reminds you that nothing can pull you out of your seat in Christ—no sin, no failure, no fear. You are anchored where He is.

Affirmation:
I am seated with Christ in heavenly places. I live from victory, not for it. I carry His peace, His perspective, and His authority into every part of my life.

Prayer:

Jesus, thank You for raising me up with You. Thank You that I'm not trying to earn a place—I already have one, right beside You. I choose to live from that reality today. Help me see from heaven's perspective, pray from heaven's authority, and walk in heaven's peace. Let my words, actions, and mindset reflect where I'm seated—not under, but above, in You. When life tries to drag me back into striving and fear, remind me that I'm already positioned in victory. I trust You, I rest in You, and I live from You. Amen.

50

HE GAVE ME THE MINISTRY OF RECONCILIATION

2 Corinthians 5:18–19 (NKJV) Now all things are of God, who has reconciled us to Himself through Jesus Christ, and has given us the ministry of reconciliation, that is, that God was in Christ reconciling the world to Himself, not imputing their trespasses to them, and has committed to us the word of reconciliation.

Romans 5:11 (NLT) So now we can rejoice in our wonderful new relationship with God because our Lord Jesus Christ has made us friends of God.

Jesus didn't just restore your relationship with God—He gave you a mission. You've been entrusted with something sacred: the ministry of reconciliation. That means your life now carries an eternal message, not of judgment, but of invitation. You get to tell the world that God is not counting their sins against them because of Jesus. That's not just good news—it's life-changing news, that's the Gospel!

Reconciliation isn't a religious duty—it's a relational call. It starts with your own restored connection with the Father, and it overflows into your relationships with others. As someone who's been brought near, you now reach out. As someone who's been embraced, you now embrace. You don't need a pulpit or platform—you are the message. Through your kindness, your peace, your forgiveness, and your story, you show people what God is really like.

Every interaction becomes an opportunity to reflect God's grace and extend His open invitation.

This calling doesn't come with pressure—it comes with joy. You're not saving the world. You're pointing to the One who already did. And you do it with love, humility, and authenticity. Whether it's a conversation, a prayer, a listening ear, or an act of grace, every moment can carry the fragrance of reconciliation. You are a minister, not because you earned it, but because you received it.

You're not just forgiven—you are sent. You're not just loved—you are commissioned. You are a walking invitation to the world: "Come home to God, He's not mad at you, He's not holding your sins against you, it's safe to come to Him."

Affirmation: I have been reconciled to God, and I carry the ministry of reconciliation. I am a living invitation to others to experience His love and grace.

Prayer: Father, thank You for restoring me to Yourself through Jesus. Thank You that I am not just saved but sent. I receive the ministry of reconciliation as a joyful privilege, not a burden. Help me represent Your heart clearly—with truth, compassion, and gentleness. Let my words bring hope and my actions reflect Your kindness. Make me a bridge for others to find their way home to You. Amen.

51

HE MADE ME A VESSEL OF HIS GLORY

2 Corinthians 4:7 (NKJV) But we have this treasure in earthen vessels, that the excellence of the power may be of God and not of us.

John 17:22 (NIV) I have given them the glory that you gave me, that they may be one as we are one.

God didn't just save you—He filled you. He placed something eternal, beautiful, and powerful within you: His own Spirit. His glory is not a cloud above or a place you visit—it's a treasure within you. And not because you earned it, but because He wanted to make His home in you. You are a carrier of heaven on earth, a vessel of divine light in a fragile human frame.

What you carry is not fragile—it's eternal. The treasure inside of you is stronger than the trials around you. You may not always feel glorious, but your life is now intertwined with His presence. When the world sees weakness, God sees a willing vessel. His glory shines brightest through surrendered lives, not perfect ones.

This isn't about performance—it's about presence. You don't need a stage or a spotlight to reflect God's glory. It shows up in how you love, how you forgive, how you stay when it's hard and speak life when it's easier to criticize. You may feel ordinary, but the glory inside you is extraordinary. Christ has given you His glory—not for status, but for unity, transformation, and witness. You are proof that God chooses the humble and lowly to display His greatness. His presence in you is the evidence of His nearness to the world.

Wherever you go, the glory goes. His Spirit in you makes every place you walk holy ground. Whether you're praying, working, parenting, creating, or resting—God is expressing His glory through your yielded heart. You are not empty—you are filled. You are not common—you are consecrated. You are not insignificant—you are radiant with the very presence of God.

Affirmation: I am a vessel of God's glory. His treasure lives in me. I carry His presence everywhere I go.

Prayer: Father, thank You for placing Your glory in me. Thank You for trusting me with Your Spirit and power. I may be an earthen vessel, but what You've put in me is priceless. Let Your glory shape how I think, how I speak, and how I show up in the world.

Teach me to live with holy awareness, to honor what I carry, and to walk in a way that reflects You. Help me remember that my worth isn't in what others see — it's in the treasure You've placed within me. Let Your glory shine through my life — boldly, humbly, and with joy. I want to reflect You everywhere I go. Amen.

52

HE WILL GLORIFY ME WITH HIM FOREVER

Romans 8:30 (NKJV) Moreover whom He predestined, these He also called; whom He called, these He also justified; and whom He justified, these He also glorified.

John 17:24 (CSB) Father, I want those you have given me to be with me where I am, so that they will see my glory, which you have given me because you loved me before the world's foundation.

The story doesn't end here. Just as Jesus was glorified after His resurrection, you too will share in His glory for eternity. This isn't a vague hope—it's a divine promise. God's plan for you is complete: He called you, justified you, and already sees you glorified. In His eternal perspective, your future is as certain as the cross and the empty tomb. You're not waiting to see if you'll make it—you're walking toward a glory already secured.

Jesus longs for you to be with Him—not merely as a distant admirer, but as a glorified son or daughter standing beside Him, radiant in shared beauty and love. He prayed that you would see His glory, not just from afar, but as one who belongs there. That is your destiny—to be with Him where He is, clothed in His righteousness, reflecting His majesty.

This hope doesn't remove the hardships of life, but it reshapes them. Every trial you endure, every tear you cry, and every act of faith in the face of pain is storing up a "far more exceeding and eternal weight of glory" (2 Corinthians 4:17). You are being prepared for something beyond imagination—full union, full joy, and full glory with Christ forever.

Eternal life isn't just about endless existence—it's about unending fellowship with Jesus. He will glorify you with His own glory, the very glory the Father gave Him. You are not just saved—you are destined to shine. This promise lifts your perspective, anchors your heart, and fuels your hope. Let it shape your priorities. Let it soften your pain. Let it strengthen your joy.

Affirmation: I have been called, justified, and glorified in Christ. I will live with Him and share in His glory forever.

Prayer: Jesus, thank You for the promise of glory. Thank You that my story ends in Your presence—whole, radiant, and forever secure. You've written the ending, and it is beautiful. Let this hope rise in my heart when life feels heavy. Help me live with my eyes on eternity, knowing that every step I take here is leading me closer to You. I look forward to the day I see You face to face and share fully in what You've prepared. Let that hope fill me with courage, strength, and joy today. Amen.

CONCLUSION

As you come to the end of this book, I want to leave you with a heartfelt encouragement. Everything you've read—every promise, every passage, every finished work of Jesus—is more than information. It is living truth, designed by God to take root in your heart and produce fruit that looks like His kingdom.

Jesus said that when His Word is planted in the soil of a believing heart, it grows up and bears fruit thirty, sixty, and even a hundredfold. That's what I pray for you. These truths are not just for study; they are for transformation. They are seeds of life and power that will shape how you think, how you see yourself, and how you respond to the world around you.

I encourage you to return to these pages often. Let this book become a tool for renewing your mind and strengthening your faith. Read until these promises become believable to you. Meditate until your heart is persuaded. Allow the Spirit of God to make your new nature in Christ more real to you than your old ways of thinking or living.

Remember, you are His workmanship. You are not trying to become something; you already are a new creation in Christ Jesus. Every day is an opportunity to put on that new self, to live in the awareness of what Jesus accomplished for you in His death, burial, and resurrection, and to walk boldly as a child of God.

The abundant life Jesus promised is not a distant hope—it is present reality. It is yours now. As you keep your heart open to the Word, you'll find yourself thriving in His peace, His joy, and His victory. And as that life overflows, you will naturally shine as a light in the world, pointing others to the goodness and grace of our Savior.

So decide today, and again tomorrow, and every day after: to believe, to receive, and to walk in all that Jesus has already done for you. The world needs the Christ in you. Live from that truth, and let your life become living proof of His finished work.

ABOUT THE AUTHOR

Clint Byars is the lead pastor of Forward Church in Sharpsburg, Georgia. With a message rooted in the finished work of Jesus and the believer's identity in Christ, Clint's passion is to help people experience lasting transformation by renewing the mind and persuading the heart with truth.

His teaching blends biblical theology with practical tools for spiritual growth, often integrating insights from neuroscience, quantum physics, and emotional healing. Clint's approach is both revelatory and grounded—anchored in Scripture, yet boldly exploring how God's Word brings life to every part of our being.

Through books, sermons, and ministry training, Clint empowers believers to live from the Spirit, walk in the fullness of grace, and participate in God's kingdom with joy and purpose. He and his wife Sara lead Forward Church together, raising up a community of believers who are rooted in love, grounded in grace, and equipped to impact the world. Find more resources from Clint at **clintbyars.com** or forward.church. Enroll in courses at www.forwardschooloftransformation.com.

MORE BOOKS BY CLINT BYARS

Devil Walk: A True Story of Drugs, Demonic Possession, and Deliverance

Who Do You Love?: Discover How to Live *from* Purpose and Fulfill Your Call

Chosen and Loved: Healing for the Hurting, Rejected, and Overlooked

Paul's Prophetic Lens: Paul's Journey to Faith-Righteousness through the Law and Prophets

Seeds of Prosperity: A Workbook for Planting God's Financial Wisdom in Your Heart

God Says Yes to Over 3000 Promises

In Christ: A Meditation Devotional In Your New Creation Identity In Christ

www.ingramcontent.com/pod-product-compliance
Lightning Source LLC
Chambersburg PA
CBHW051835090426
42736CB00011B/1808